Cyborg Anthropology

Cyborg Anthropology

Theological Engagement with
Posthuman Discourses

Merin Mathew

Christian World Imprints

First Published in 2020 by

Christian World Imprints
Christian Publishing & Books from India
C-3, Wazirpur Industrial Area
Delhi-110052
cwidelhi2017@gmail.com
www.ChristianWorldImprints.com
Phone: +91 11 41526079

ISBN: 978-93-5148-497-4

Printed in India.

Dedication

In Memory of Rev. Dr. Geevarughese Mathew (1949-2019), Former Principal of the Mar Thoma Theological Seminary and Professor of Old Testament. He was a compassionate teacher, spiritual mentor and a great human being.

The book in its original form is the thesis submitted to the Senate of Serampore College, towards the M.Th. Degree 2019 and the Original Title is **"Theological Anthropology in the Context of Cyberspace: A Search for an Authentic Christian Human Formation."** It is published with written permission from the Senate of Serampore. The author is responsible for the title, contents and opinions expressed in it.

Contents

Foreword

Love it or loathe it, we are all cyborg beings! Our lives have embraced and have been impacted by technology with all its complexities. For some, the cyborg and the human are harmonious entities; and for some, bringing a theological formulation to explain the embeddedness of technology in our lives does not sit well in the so-understood spiritual realms. Therefore, there are ongoing theological struggles surrounding the debates on the created and the manufactured.

Rev. Merin Matthew's work comes to us as a refreshing research-based conversation addressing the love-loathe relationship between technology and theology. The book offers greater currency to the debates on Cyborg and its Christian theological relevance. It questions unhelpful—and at times denigrating—anthropocentric attitudes our spiritualities and theological discourses uncritically uphold. It does so by answering the questions like: What constitutes the human from the vantage point of the Image of God (Imago Dei) in the context of cyberspace and its challenges for the conventional premise of theological anthropology. Importantly, it also addresses how at the core of Christological formulations is a call for a deep hybridity of entities that are often deemed incompatibles.

At the heart of the investigation is the argument that warns us of detachments either from technology at the expense of humans or from humans at the expense of technology. In fact, the notion of the extremes of cyborgs points to the spectrum of our attitudes to technological developments spanning between the heartening life-enhancing possibilities and the dangerous notion of extermination. I certainly appreciate Merin for embarking on a challenging and rare thesis topic at Masters level and for sharing his wisdom through this book.

In fact, at the heart of Merin's wider theological conversations is the zeal and boldness to relate to life some untouched theological debates. His enthusiasm and inquisitiveness have made him explore newer ideas. These explorations could be found in his Bible studies, the training programmes he conducts and in the regular conversations that he most often initiates or constructively contributes to. He has made an impacting presence on social media by striking a delicate balance between high theological jargons and their common parlance. I have had the joy of engaging in such conversations with him and also about football, food and other routines of life.

When I first got to go through Merin's thesis proposal, I was thoroughly excited for the prospects it offered. I was able to see that Merin was charting some stimulating directions in faith construction and its process in relation to a rare field of Cyborg discourse. It was my joy to journey with him in his research and writing process. All these make me delighted to recommend Merin's work *Cyborg Anthropology: Theological Engagement with Posthuman Discourses* for its insights on Cyborg Anthropology and its engagement with theological themes such as *Imago Dei*, and also for their deep connections to Christology at fundamental levels.

Rev. Dr. Rohan P. Gideon
Associate Professor, Christian Theology
The United Theological College
Bengaluru
22nd August 2020

Acknowledgement

It is with great joy that I acknowledge certain people and institutions who have helped in this book come to fruition. Primarily, I thank the Mar Thoma Church that I belong to, for giving me the opportunity to pursue my Master of Theology (M.Th.) from United Theological College, Bengaluru. The opportunity to study has been hugely rewarding and a blessing. My utmost gratitude to Most Rev Dr Joseph Mar Thoma Metropolitan and all the Bishops.

I was fortunate to study in the department of Christian Theology and Ethics in United Theological College. Rev Dr R. Sahayadhas has been very instrumental in my research work and helped me to have a focused methodology in the writing period. His inspiring guidance and urge for clarity has been very central and the entire study period has been filled with hospitality and care along with the academic rigour. The pastoral element of thesis writing and theological studies has been very well been on the centre stage, thanks to Dr Sahayadhas.

My guide Rev Dr Rohan Gideon has been a constant inspiration and energy behind this study. The process of writing this research work was very rewarding as Dr Gideon was compassionate as a person and focused with regards to content. The suggestion of revision of my drafts were done with great sensitivity without compromising on the message that more is expected in the articulations. The many conversations with him have been very fruitful and his directions to contact the right people and right books have been astonishing. His promptness and detailed comments have been a huge learning experience for me. He has been very kind and generous to write a Foreword for this book, which I am deeply grateful for.

Dr George Zachariah, who was the Professor of Ethics at UTC has been a constant guide in the process of my studies and his conversations and guidance on the topic have been very important. My deepest gratitude to him for pointing me to the right resource materials. I deem it my great privilege to be taught my Rev Dr Christopher Duraisingh for one semester. With his erudition and precision he helped me expand the horizons of the thesis.

My special appreciation also to the Librarian Mrs Susan Daniel and the staff of UTC Libray. The promptness with which the Librarian ordered some of the books necessary for my Thesis, was very helpful. Also most of my writing has been done at the library, and therefore it has been my sacred space for daily encounters of encouragement and correction.

Thanks to my guide Dr Gideon, I could get in touch with Dr Scott Midson, who is a Faculty at University of Manchester and author of the book "Cyborg Theology: Humans, Technology and God." He was kind to go through my core arguments and make some critical corrections in the initial phase. Indeed, I am very grateful.

Rev Sam Koshy T., who is currently a research scholar in the Early Church at University of Bern, Switzerland has been instrumental in directing me to the topic selected and has been a constant conversation partner throughout the period of thesis writing. He has also been instrumental in getting key resources. Rev Prince Varghese who is doing his Ph.D. in Practical Theology from Princeton Theological Seminary, New Jersey has been also instrumental in getting access to key journal articles.

My classmates of the Theology department have been a constant support, as our conversations and encouragements were very critical. My special appreciation to the Batch of 2017-19 (M.Th) as they all have been very instrumental in the process.

My appreciation to Rev Dr Santanu K. Patro, the Dean of the Senate of Serampore, for giving permission to publish my thesis as a book.

Mr Sudhanshu Kanda of Christian World Imprints has been very approachable and has been a good guide in helping me to realize the output of the thesis as a monograph. My appreciation to his wife Anshul Kanda and the Editorial Team for doing great job with the manuscript and the layout.

I am deeply grateful to the Principal of Dhrama Jyoti Vidya Peeth, Rev Dr Sunni E. Mathew and my fellow faculty members for the encouragement and collegiality I have been blessed to be part of. I express my gratitude to the students of Dharma Jyoti.

I also thank my cousin Rev Jobin E. T. Abraham, for the wonderful coverpage and the many options he gave me to choose.

Soji's parents and my parents have been a very constant support during my studies and specifically during the thesis writing. Their unconditional love and encouragement has been an oasis.

My wife Soji has been my strength, my counsellor, my encourager throughout the process. She knew when I was tensed and when I was relaxed and always motivated me if I went through a rough patch, which I often went through. She meticulously read my draft and helped with proof reading. Her prayers, her understanding and her affirmations I am eternally grateful for.

I, most importantly thank the Triune God revealed in Jesus Christ "For in him we live and move and have our being" (Acts 17:28).

Abbreviations

A.I.	Artificial Intelligence
C.C.C.	Created Co-Creator
Col	Colossians
Cor	Corinthians
Creatio Continua-	Latin for 'Continuous Creation'
Creatio Ex Nihilo-	Latin for 'Creation from Nothing'
Gen	Genesis
H+	Humanity Plus
Imago Dei	Image of God
F.A.Q.	Frequently Asked Questions
Mt	Matthew
Mic	Micah
M.U.D.	Multi-User Dungeon
N.A.B.	New American Bible
N.B.I.C.	Nanotechnology, Biotechnology, Information Technology and Cognitive Science
N.I.V.	New International Version
P2P	Peer to Peer
Sci-Fi-	Scientific Fiction
Tikkun Olam-	Hebrew for mending the broken world.
W.C.C.	World Council of Churches
W.T.A.	World Transhumanist Association

Introduction

In the Sci-fi genre, the concept of Cyborg is very popular. Many movies, especially the Avenger Series and Iron Man series from the Marvel Studio, have triggered popular imagination beyond just intellectual speculations. But, then what is a Cyborg? How do we understand a Human Being? How does one engage in a Cyberspace with conventional Theological Anthropology?

The study is a nuanced search in the larger debate of Science and Religion called the Theology and Technology studies. Technology has been instrumental and aided the Lutheran Reformation, thanks to the Guttenberg's Printing Press which hugely accelerated the phenomenon and provided Bibles for personal reading. But since then, or historically it could be the Puritan Movement which pictured technology either as an aberration or just for functional purpose. The human/technology binary has been profound as at a popular level, Churches have denounced television, mass media, computers, internet, cell phones and what not. But, in the context of Covid 19, one realizes that cyberspace has opened up a new understanding of human being itself with multiple technologies enabling virtual gatherings and possibilities of being a Church. The study engages with Cyberspace and sees how the conventional understanding of a human being is not helpful in our engagement. The conventional understanding of humans as distinct, superior and pure, and the world of technology as something for the benefit humans is an obsolete paradigm. The understanding of humans as Cyborg can seem troublesome and also problematic. But, certain transgressions in theology lead to a deeper engagement. The researcher wishes to root the discourse of Cyborg in the framework of Posthumanism over Transhumanism and the reason for it will be elaborated in the course of the research work. Humans as hybrid who are created co-creators is what the researcher attempts to explore. The search also attempts to understand various doctrines in engagement with cyberspace as doctrines help in human formation. Therefore, the glorification of technology at the expense of humans or glorification of humans at the expense of technology are two paradigms that exist. The researcher says that such a binary is faulty. The Cyborg Anthropology is a paradigm of engagement which resists any of the extreme trends.

In the first chapter the researcher is aware that there are two predominant binaries in the approach of technology. One is technophobia and the other is technophilia. The two important strands of philosophical discourses with technology are Transhumanism and the other being Posthumanism. The researcher attempts to strike a corollary suitable to engage with theological anthropology.

The second Chapter the researcher surveys different typologies of *Imago Dei*. There are 3 typologies namely a) Substantial, b) Functional and c) Relational. In consideration with the engagement points of technology for a human, the best among the three is chosen.

The third chapter is about the methodology employed. The larger framework of hybridity is employed and Philip Hefner's paradigm of "Created Co-Creator" is explored for a creative conversation between theology and technology.

The fourth chapter is a theological engagement with specific emphasis on Christology in reimagining with the conversation of a Cyborg Anthropology. The conviction of the researcher is that a healthy Christology helps in a mature formulation of theological anthropology in the context of cyberspace.

Chapter 1

Searching the Anthropological Corollary in the Context of Cyberspace

Introduction

In the dialogue between Theology and Technology, it has become very imperative to understand the evolution of the concept of human being in the context of cyberspace. The philosophical paradigm to engage with Cyberspace will be the focus of this chapter. The researcher with the question of "What is the concept of 'human being' in cyberspace?" wishes to explore the Posthuman discourse in search of an appropriate anthropological corollary to the theological anthropological debate of *Imago Dei* which will be dealt in the next chapter. It now becomes imperative to define and understand cyberspace.

1.1. Defining Cyberspace

There are multiple definitions of cyberspace. Cees J. Hamelink defines it as "Virtual communicative space created by digital technologies. It is not limited to the operation of computer networks, but also encompasses all social activities in which digital information and communication technologies are deployed."[1] David Bell elaborates,

> First, cyberspace can be seen as the material components that provide a communications infrastructure allowing various forms of interaction between parties. Secondly, cyberspace can be seen as the symbolic, imagined space between nodes on the network that allows new selves and new worlds to be created. Finally, cyberspace can be seen as experiential, whereby the interaction of material and symbolic components defines the kind of experience.[2]

Based on the above definition and observations it is evident that cyberspace is an important context. The integrated and layered dimension of cyberspace shows that it contributes to the formative and creative aspects of human life. Mbasasano opines that "Cyberspace results from the human collective ability to articulate possibilities in which technological artefacts are designed, used, and conceptualized as artifacts that are mechanical or computational creations, ranging from simple tools, complex devices, computer software, virtual reality, cybernetics, virtual reality and beyond."[3] Cyberspace cannot be reduced to just internet, but there is a need to understand complex ecology consisting of devices, gadgets of evolving generation, wired and non-wired prosthetics and the way body adjusts or adapts to this space.

---

[1] Cees J. Hamelink, *The Ethics of Cyberspace* (New Delhi: Sage Publications, 2000), ix.

[2] David Bell, *An Introduction to Cybercultures* (New York: Routledge, 2001), 6-7.

[3] U. M. Mbanaso, "The Cyberspace: Redefining A New World," *IOSR Journal of Computer Engineering* (IOSR-JCE) Vol. 17, Issue 3, Ver. VI (May – Jun 2015), 19.

1.1.1. Understanding Authenticity

Continuing with the above strand of thought, one realizes that the question of authenticity[4] is a debate in the realm of cyberspace with the distinction of real-virtual binary. There has been much contention whether social actions within cyberspace have the same quality as face-to-face interactions. Kerstin Rade-Antweiler says,

> The first question deals whether people's experiences, as well as their virtual bodies, can be considered authentic or real online. Connected with this, the second theme concerns the definition of the environment itself, considering whether cyberspace is a 'real,' authentic space. It becomes clear that both topics are based on the distinction and definition of the terms 'online' and 'offline,' or 'real' and 'virtual.'[5]

This helps in understanding that the subject is more nuanced than assumed earlier. L. L. Dawson stresses the ambiguity of online activity as different and at the same time similar to offline experiences, which are identified by him as the "real" experiences.[6] So, how does one understand the dichotomy between virtual[7] and real? Deleuze saw cyberspace as an integral part of reality

---

[4] Originally the term "authenticity" was derived from the Greek *auto* and *entes,* and meant, "to fulfill something in oneself." Cf., Kerstin Rade-Antweiler, "Authenticity" in *Digital Religion: Understanding Religious Practice in New Media World,* edited by Heidi A. Campbell, (New York: Routlege, 2013), 88.

[5] Kerstin Rade-Antweiler, "Authenticity" in *Digital Religion: Understanding Religious Practice in New Media World,* edited by Heidi A. Campbell, (New York: Routledge, 2013), 88.

[6] L. L. Dawson, "Researching Religion in Cyberspace: Issues and Strategies," in *Religion on the Internet: Research Prospects and Promises,* edited by J. K. Hadden and D. E. Cowan (New York: Elsevier Science, 2000), 28.

[7] Antweiler quotes Baudrillard "In this perspective, virtual worlds are seen as mere simulations, as stressed by Baudrillard (1994) in his theory of simulation. According to him, it has become impossible to distinguish between the original and a copy, reality and fiction, model and image, due to the fact that the images of reality are nowadays portrayed primarily through mass media, and have become more important and powerful than the reality itself. Thus the world presented by the media is a simulated, illusory world, what Baudrillard defines as the "simulacrum,"

and replaced the binary "virtual" and "real" with "virtual" versus "actual."[8] He pointed out that virtuality can be considered as complete and real, and "must be defined as strictly a part of the real object"[9] The qualifications such as "virtual," "real" or "authentic" depend totally on users' understanding: "What happens in virtual worlds often is just as real, just as meaningful to participants in cyberspace"[10] For many users, their offline and online lives are seen as contexts that are merged and interwoven, they are not seen as contradictory. As Boellstorff stresses: "What makes these virtual worlds real is that relationships, romance, economic transactions, and community take place with them – in short, that they are places of human culture. It is this social reality that links virtual and actual."[11] So, the researcher affirms that conventional dichotomy of real versus virtual is superflous and cyberspace is seen as a space where authentic experiences and formations are possible and need serious engagement.

1.1.2. Inhabiting Cyberspace

As the authenticity is established, it becomes pertinent to know whether words like inhabiting that one uses for so called "real" spaces can be likewise used for cyberspace. Mario E. Tosello says,

> It is usual to develop some kind of activity in cyberspace, so one can say that we inhabit digital environments in certain way, since the verb to inhabit refers to the relationship and interaction we establish with our "world." To inhabit is related with our customs, our habits and therefore we realize, the words inhabit and habit are intertwined. Since inhabiting cyberspace has

---

which captures the real world in the form of a hyper-reality." See Kerstin Rade-Antweiler, "Authenticity" in *Digital Religion,* 94.

[8] Kerstin Rade-Antweiler, "Authenticity" in *Digital Religion,* 95.

[9] Gilles Deleuze, *Difference and Repetition* (London: Continuum, 2004), 260.

[10] T. L. Taylor, *Play Between Worlds: Exploring Online Game Culture* (Cambridge, MA: MIT Press, 2006), 1.

[11] Tom Boellstorff, *Coming of Age in Second Life: An Anthropologist Explores the Virtually Human* (NJ: Princeton University Press, 2008), 245.

> become part of our habits, of our way to inhabit, the digital environment has been incorporated into our human environment.[12]

It is clear that cyberspace brings about a different bodily disposition where habits orient us differently and formatively. Therefore, one can talk about cyberspace as a *habitus*[13] to engage with. But cyberspace, as virtual space, opens a new observation and experimentation of space, therefore it needs a different conceptualization and a new understanding of the concept of human. Noreen Herzfeld observes that "Digital spaces are built on data. These spaces can be moving and transforming if the data change. In such cases, cyberspace is not only moving but changing itself, because the data that gives the birth are varying constantly."[14] Elaine Graham analyses "Space is here like a living thing that grows, moves, and creates an ever-changing landscape. This fact is only possible in cyberspace, and the result is a nomadic and metamorphic understanding of human. In digital space we can think about a new kind of human which some have tried to term as posthuman."[15] Based on Herzfeld and Graham's observations, it is clear that inhabiting cyberspace is conceptually possible which brings a more textured understanding and therefore the posthuman discourse will be needed to involve with.

---

[12] Mario E. Tosello, "Performing Cyberspace: Dance, Technology and Virtual Architecture," *International Journal of Architectural Computing*, Issue 03, Vol. 01 (2003), 395.

[13] The concept of Habitus is very central in the theory of Bourdieu. Through the concepts of habitus and desire one gets a strong sense of dialectical process whereby social practices are incorporated within the body only then to be reproduced by way of embodied activity. The centrality of Bourdiean emphasis is the centrality of practice or human action. This is what concept of habitus is designed to achieve. Cf., Nick Crossley, *Social Bodies: Habit, Identity and Desire* (London: Sage Publications, 2001), 92.

[14] Noreen Herzfeld, *Technology and Religion: Remaining Human in a Co-created World* (West Conshohocken, PA: Templeton Press, 2009), 56.

[15] Elaine L. Graham, *Representations of the Post/Human: Monsters, Aliens and Others in Popular Culture* (New Jersey: Rutgers University Press, 2002), 1.

1.1.3. On Being Human in Cyberspace

"What it means to be a human?" in the context of cyberspace is an integral question. Understanding cyberspace as *Habitus* means to know the embodiment of humans with artifacts in the given context. Gray helps in understanding that "The 'worlds' engendered by the creative imagination in myth, language and religion, are just as revealing, in their own way, of the ethical and political dimensions of the digital and biotechnological age as conventionally are the material artefacts of humanity's technological endeavours."[16] This makes clear there are some fluidities and continuities between cyberspace and material conventional spaces. John Harris adds a poignant point. "So what needs to be explored is that how new technologies along with adding new patterns of work, leisure and social interaction, have called into question or contested the immutability of boundaries between humans, animals and machines, 'born' and 'made.'"[17] Graham sums it up well by saying,

> In challenging the fixity of 'human nature', the digital and biotechnological and cyberspace age engenders revisiting of the basic assumptions on which matters such as personal identity, the configuration of community, the grounds of human uniqueness and the relationship between body and mind.[18]

So, the discontinuities as expressed by Harris and Graham have called into question the distinctive identity of humans where the uniqueness is seen more as a construct assuming privileges of power. It is here that the discourse of posthumanism for a corollary anthropology becomes relevant.

---

[16] Chris Habbles Gray, *Cyborg Citizen: Politics in Posthuman Age* (New York: Routledge, 2001), 3.

[17] John Harris, *Clones, Genes and Immortality* (Oxford: Oxford University Press, 1998), viii.

[18] Elaine L. Graham, *Representations of the Post/Human,* 1-2.

1.2. What is Posthumanism?

Posthumanism brings a unique vantage point to the debate in the context of cyberspace. Cary Wolfe writes, "Posthumanism names a historical moment in which the decentering of the human by its imbrication in technical, cyber-virtual, medical, informatics, and economic networks is increasingly impossible to ignore."[19] Although, 'posthumanism' is a notably broad and perhaps too encompassing term, Pramod Nayyar says that "The consensus on the emerging field of study is that it addresses technologies, or at least dynamism highlighted in a techno-cultural context, and how these change our conceptions of humans and others."[20] For Wolfe, this suggests a decentering of the human, which is a significant strand of posthumanism, but it is important to realize that it is not the only strand. Posthuman is not singular, posthuman is inevitably plural. Brent Waters says, "The plasticity of human nature which engenders posthuman speculation regarding humanity's future selves also ensures that uniformity is hardly to be expected in whatever possible forms the future may take."[21]

The researcher would like to employ the posthuman discourse to critically interrogate the concept of human nature itself. Questions like 'Is there something like essential human nature?' 'What kind of anthropology emerges in the discourse of cyberspace?' and 'What kind of a vision of human in the changing context does one envisage?' Francesca Ferrando says, "There is an ontological category of human that needs to be looked into that assumes that the boundaries that define the human is constructed, which needs a conscious and conscientious deliberation for the same."[22] So, posthumanism does address the complexities of an ethos filled with

---

[19] Cary Wolfe, *What is Posthumanism?* (Minneapolis: University of Minnesota Press, 2009), xv.

[20] Pramod K. Nayar, *Posthumanism* (Cambridge: Polity Press, 2014), 2.

[21] Brent Waters, *From Human to Posthuman: Christian Theology and Technology in a Postmodern World* (Hampshire: Ashgate, 2006), 50.

[22] Francesca Ferrando, "The Posthuman: Philosophical Posthumanism and Its Others" (Ph.D. dissertation, Università di Roma Tre, 2014), 17.

gadgets and prosthetics that decenters the earlier held understanding of personhood.

Jeanine Thweatt-Bates says that "Posthuman as it is currently used may sometimes refer to transhumanist ideas of posthuman future, in a sort of humanism-plus. It may also refer to anti-human or critical posthumanism constructions within what Stephen Garner characterizes as 'narratives of apprehension.'"[23] Considering 'Cyborg' and 'Uploads' as competing and multiple notions of Posthuman, Bates says, "The cyborg is a posthuman feminist construction, birthed in the landmark essay referred to in shorthand as the 'A Cyborg Manifesto,' by Donna J. Haraway… in which the hybrid embodiment of the cyborg serves as a symbol for the ontological kinship of the human with the posthuman."[24] Thweatt-Bates contends that considering posthumanism as a homogenous concept is detrimental to the theological task. She describes "'Cyborg'[25] refers specifically to Haraway's Posthuman construction to be categorized under Postfoundationalism[26], and 'Upload'[27] to a specific Transhumanist posthuman construction.[28] Researcher will discuss Cyborg under Postfoundationalism and Upload along with other stands of Transhumanism, to choose an anthropology for cyberspace. Transhumanism will be first explored.

---

[23] Jeanine Thweatt-Bates, *Cyborg Selves: A Theological Anthropology of the Posthuman* (London and New York: Routledge, Taylor and Francis Group, 2012), 5.

[24] Jeanine Thweatt- Bates, *Cyborg Selves,* 5.

[25] Cyborg is a feminist posthuman construction, birthed in the landmark essay "A Cyborg Manifesto" by Donna J. Haraway. The hybrid embodiment of the cyborg serves as a symbol for the ontological kinship of the human with the nonhuman. See Jeanine Thweatt- Bates, *Cyborg Selves,* 5.

[26] Jeanine Thweatt- Bates, *Cyborg Selves,* 11.

[27] Uploaded consciousness is a transhumanist construction, proposed as a desirable but still theoretical possibility for shedding the biological body for a virtual existence or a more durable artificial body. See Jeanine Thweatt- Bates, *Cyborg Selves,* 5.

[28] Jeanine Thweatt- Bates, *Cyborg Selves,* 5.

1.3. Transhumanism

Researcher is aware of the merits of Transhumanism but will carefully tread to analyse and understand before choosing Cyborg and its layered debate.

World Transhumanist Association (W.T.A.)[29] defines transhumanism as,

> 1) The intellectual and cultural movement that affirms the possibility and desirability of fundamentally improving the human condition through applied reason, especially by developing widely available technologies by eliminating aging and to greatly enhance human intellectual, physical and psychological capacities. 2)) The study of the ramifications, promises, and potential dangers of technologies that will enable us to overcome fundamental human limitations, and the related study of the ethical matters involved in developing and using such technologies.[30]

Hughes elaborates the vision as "The aim is not be well, but 'better than well'[31] by using technologies to transcend the human limitation of embodiment that has a vision of life without aging, disease, pain and suffering."[32] Bostrom says "Transhumanists place a high value on autonomy: the ability and right of individuals to plan and choose their own lives."[33] Researcher understands that

---

[29] The WTA is now known as Humanity+, See "Transhumanist FAQ," accessed 3 Nov 2018, https://humanityplus.org/philosophy/transhumanist-faq/

[30] Nick Bostrom, "Introduction-The Transhumanist FAQ: A General Introduction," in *Transhumanism and the Body: The World Religion Speaks*, edited by Calvin Mercer and Derek F. Maher (New York: Palgrave Macmillan, 2004), 1.

[31] The Slogan "better than well" is integral feature of the Humanity+ See "Transhumanist FAQ," accessed 3 Nov 2018, https://humanityplus.org/philosophy/transhumanist-faq/

[32] James Hughes, *Citizen Cyborg: Why Democratic Societies Must Respond to the Redesigned Human of the Future* (Cambridge, MA: Westview Press, 2004), 156.

[33] Nick Bostrom, The Transhumanist FAQ: A General Introduction, Version 2.1, World Transhumanist Association, October 2003, accessed 3 Nov 2018, https://nickbostrom.com/views/transhumanist.pdf.

Trashumanism has continuity with Enlightenment philosophy. Bostrom summarizes,

> The heritage from the Renaissance combines with the influences of Isaac Newton, Thomas Hobbes, John Locke, Immanuel Kant, Marquis de Condorcet, and others to form the basis for rational humanism, which emphasizes science and critical reasoning – rather than revelation and religious authority – as ways of learning about the natural world and the destiny and nature of man and of providing a grounding for morality. Transhumanism traces its roots to this rational humanism.[34]

Transhumanism in the realm of technology and cyberspace is seen as 'humanity plus' "where goals of enhancement explicitly include the pursuit of longevity and the elimination of aging, disease, pain and suffering."[35] It is therefore imperative to understand the different strands of Transhumanism at this juncture.

1.3.1. The Upload Scenario

Bates as seen earlier says Upload and Cyborg are two important strands in Posthumanism. Researcher wishes to see whether it would be compatible with the larger goal. Bostrom says "Uploading[36] is the process of transferring an intellect from a biological brain to a computer."[37] Ray Kurzweil describes uploading as a process of "scanning all of the salient details and then reinstating those details into a suitably powerful computational substrate. This process would capture a person's entire personality, memory, skills, and history."[38] Bostrom says "This of course is a speculative possibility that would

---

[34] Nick Bostrom, The Transhumanist FAQ: A General Introduction, Version 2.1, accessed 3 Nov 2018.

[35] Jeanine Thweatt- Bates, *Cyborg Selves,* 44.

[36] This is also referred to as "downloading". "mind uploading," and "brain reconstruction." See Nick Bostrom, The Transhumanist FAQ, accessed 5 Nov 2018.

[37] Nick Bostrom, The Transhumanist FAQ: A General Introduction, Version 2.1, accessed 5 Nov 2018.

[38] Ray Kurzweil, *The Singularity is Near: When Humans Transcend Biology* (New York: Penguin Books, 2005), 198-99.

require progress both in neuroscience, to develop an adequately detailed three-dimensional map of the brain as well as adequate computing capacity, in order to run the upload to interact with the external world or with a virtual reality."[39] However, extrapolating from the exponential rapidity of technological advances in scanning and sensing tools and anticipating the advent of nanotechnology, Kurzweil predicts that the technology for scanning from within the brain using nanobots[40] will be available by the late 2020s, the basic computational resources by the early 2030s, and the successful uploading will take place by the end of 2030s.[41] FAQ states,

> 1) Uploads would not be subject to biological senescence. 2) Back-up copies of uploads could be created regularly so that you could be rebooted if something bad happened. (Thus your lifespan would potentially be as long as the universe's.) 3) You could potentially live much more economically as an upload since you wouldn't need physical food, housing, transportation, etc.[42]

With the rapid growth in cyberspace and technology, the above scenario of Upload looks plausible. Researcher understands that this is a much unbridled freedom premise of Enlightenment Philosophy that denigrates body and emphasizes the superiority of the mind. The anthropology expressed in this strand, the researcher reckons is not compatible with the vision of the research and therefore will not be employed in the ongoing conversation.

---

[39] Nick Bostrom, The Transhumanist FAQ: A General Introduction, Version 2.1, accessed 5 Nov 2018.

[40] Nanobots are robots that are microscopic in nature, measured largely on the scale of nanometers. They are currently in the research and development phase, but on realization they are expected to do specific tasks at the atomic, molecular and cellular level and help in bringing about many breakthroughs, especially in medical science and cyberspace. See "Nanobots," accessed 23 Jan 2019, https://www.techopedia.com/definition/8494/nanobot

[41] Ray Kurzweil, *The Singularity is Near,* 200.

[42] Nick Bostrom, The Transhumanist FAQ: A General Introduction, Version 2.1, accessed 5 Nov 2018.

1.3.2. Democratic Transhumanism[43]

The Democratic Transhumanism espouses that technology and cyberspace will increase the choices in human life and therefore increasing the happiness quotient. James Hughes says,

> Democratic transhumanism stems from the assertion that human beings will generally be happier when they take rational control of the natural and social forces that control their lives. This fundamental humanistic assertion has led to two intertwined sets of Enlightenment values: the democratic tradition with its values of liberty, equality, solidarity and collective self-governance, and to the belief in reason and scientific progress, that human beings can use reason and technology to improve the conditions of life.[44]

Bates quotes James Hughes saying,

> ... democratic transhumanism successfully addresses both the legitimate concerns of bioluddites[45] for equity, solidarity, and public safety, and libertarian concerns with our right to control our bodies and minds. Hughes in other words tries to split the difference between those who seek unregulated technological progress (extropians) and those who fear it (bioLuddites), by creating a middle ground that allows for freedom to pursue enhancement

---

[43] Democratic Transhumanism advocates both the right to use technology to transcend the limitations of the human body, and the extension of democratic concerns beyond formal legal equality and liberty into cultural and economic liberty and equality, in order to protect values such as equality, solidarity, and democratic participation in a transhuman context. See Jeanine Thweatt- Bates, *Cyborg Selves,* 48.

[44] James Hughes, "Democratic Transhumanism 2.0," Institute for Ethics and Emerging Technologies, accessed 3 Nov. 2018, https://ieet.org/index.php/IEET2/print/1339.

[45] Bioluddites are less pejoratively called the bioconservatives who fear the unrampant development of technology as a threat to humanity. See "Bioconservatives," accessed 16 Jan 2019, https://ieet.org/index.php/tpwiki/Bioconservative/.

> technologies with the provision of a certain judicious amount of regulation and universal provision.[46]

Researcher observes that the anthropology espoused by DT[47] is pretty balanced and choice based. But, the question is how will one strike the balance between the two extremes in the discourse? With the ambiguity persistent this strand does not seem to give an anthropology worthy enough to be a corollary of cyberspace.

1.3.3. Singularitarianism

With the exponential growth in the field of technology and cyberspace, one needs to have a framework of anthropology that can encompass the vision of the future. In the "Transhumanist FAQ,"[48]

> The concept of the singularity is often associated with Vernor Vinge, who regards it as one of the more probable scenarios for the future. Provided that we manage to avoid destroying civilization, Vinge thinks that a singularity is likely to happen as a consequence of advances in artificial intelligence, large systems of networked computers, computer-human integration, or some other form of intelligence amplification. Enhancing intelligence will, in this scenario, at some point lead to a positive feedback

---

[46] Jeanine Thweatt- Bates, *Cyborg Selves,* 49.

[47] Democratic Transhumanism.

[48] The Transhumanist FAQ is an important document in the history of transhumanism, covering many key matters of philosophy, politics and technology. It has been developed collaboratively since the mid-1990's to the present day by a large number of transhumanists. The FAQ is a compilation of transhumanist writings since 1989. Many of the ideas of transhumanity were covered in Extropy Institute's Extropy. The Journal of Transhumanist Thought from the late 1980s through the late 1990s, and which have been referenced in our FAQ. In order to provide state-of-the-art reliability, ExI's FAQ has been revised over the years to provide accurate answers to the crucial questions about transhumanity and the role of extropy since its earliest beginnings and it's far future. Here are many transhumanist FAQs available on the Internet. As the original transhumanist organization, Extropy Institute's goal is to provide an accurate and reliable FAQ for the growing culture of transhumanity. See "Transhumanist FAQ," accessed 26 Feb. 2019. https://hpluspedia.org/wiki/Transhumanist_FAQ .

> loop: smarter systems can design systems that are even more intelligent, and can do so more swiftly than the original human designers. This positive feedback effect would be powerful enough to drive an intelligence explosion that could quickly lead to the emergence of a superintelligent system of surpassing abilities.[49]

Vernon Vinge says, "There may be developed computers that are "awake" and superhumanly intelligent. Computer/human interfaces may become so intimate that users may reasonably be considered superhumanly intelligent."[50]

Ray Kurzweil who believes that singularity that leads to immortality says, "What's actually happening is machines are powering all of us…They're making us smarter. They may not yet be inside our bodies, but, by the 2030s, we will connect our neocortex, the part of our brain where we do our thinking, to the cloud."[51]

Researcher sees that the emerging anthropology is in the area of techno-optimism where the vision of the future is fuelled by speculations with watch words like "if we manage to avoid destroying civilization." So, the fear of inherent potential for destruction is suppressed by wishful thinking that humans will choose the better option. What will be the principles by which the humans will choose constructive approach over destructive one is not clear and such speculative vision just emphasizes the cognitive aspects while the fullness of personhood is ignored.

1.3.4. Summary

Researcher after briefly surveying the tenets of transhumanism and its strands, understands that there is an inherent techno-optimism

---

[49] Nick Bostrom, *The Transhumanist FAQ: A General Introduction*, Version 2.1, accessed 13 Dec 2018, https://nickbostrom.com/views/transhumanist.pdf.

[50] Vernon Vinge, "The Coming Technological Singularity," accessed 18 Nov. 2018, https://www.accelerating.org/articles/comingtechsingularity.html.

[51] Christina Reedy, "Kurzweil Claims That the Singularity Will Happen by 2045," *Future Society*, 5 October 2017, accessed 23 Jan 2019, https://futurism.com/kurzweil-claims-that-the-singularity-will-happen-by-2045 Quoting Kurzweil from the Interview.

which sees technology as superior which helps in overcoming the limitations of the body. The issues of immortality, future without pain and suffering, unimaginable freedom 'and progress, taking control of the future through rational choices, have been significantly emphasized. Researcher gets the feeling that the body is seen as inferior and the superiority of mind and enhancing it through technology is the major focus. Such an anthropological vision glorifies the context and undermines the agency of human beings and is seen as a subject to the evolving cyberspace which is not an ideal anthropology to engage with.

1.4. Placing the Discourse of Cyborg under Posthumanism

Cyborg[52] explained above is the Donna Haraway's concept of cyborg; the researcher will not engage with Mechanical Cyborg; Sci-Fi Cyborgs etc. The cyborg-cyberspace continuum is important which will lead to the posthuman discourse of Cyborg in the end. Bates says,

> By naming his approach "postfoundationalism," van Huyssteen signals that he seeks to negotiate a middle way between foundationalist notions of a single universal rationality, and nonfoundationalist notions of multiple, incommensurable rationalities....Huyssteen defines rationality in a way that recognizes the plurality of epistemic communities, disciplines and specific forms of rationality, but simultaneously posits an inclusive notion of "shared resources of rationality," which enables

---

[52] Ronald Kline says "The term cyborg finds its origins in the technical literature surrounding the space-race of the 1960's. Manfred Clynes and Nathan Kline coined the term 'cyborg' in their paper 'Cyborgs and Space' which was an examination of the integration of advanced technologies directly into human physiology. They imagined the cyborg as an entity who could overcome the natural limitations that prohibit humans from engaging in extended space travel. Space exploration for Clynes and Kline was a catalyst for a radical shift in how human nature and destiny were to be understood in connection with human technologies." See Ronald Kline, "Where are the Cyborg in Cybernetics?" *Social Studies of Science* 39/3 (June 2009), 331–332.

> communication across academic disciplines and specific epistemic communities.[53]

Bates continues that

> Huysteen and Haraway seek to negotiate an epistemically responsible middle way between the temptations of enlightenment objectivism and radical postmodern relativism. In doing so both thinkers emphasize the importance of the social and historical embeddedness of the embodied human knower, communal accountability, hermeneutics, and a critical realism that grants an independence to the natural world and other creatures.[54]

So, one can place the discourse of cyborg by Donna Haraway under the strand of Postfoundationalism. The basic framework of Donna Haraway needs to be placed.

1.4.1. Non-Teleological Cyborg

The researcher wishes to engage with Feminist theorist Donna Haraway's work on the symbol of cyborg in her seminal landmark essay, "A Cyborg Manifesto," which has become a reference point for discussions of posthuman.[55] Midson coined the word non-teleological cyborg to understand Haraway's cyborg. Midson says, "Haraway's cyborg rejects notions of an independent or pre-existent nature that is defined against the technologized human who distances his/herself from non-technologized 'naturalness.'"[56] Midson further states "We cannot, in short, idealise or envision any normative or innocent aspects of humanness. The non-teleological cyborg is without origin or salvific ends that reflect that origin, as both conceptual points

---

[53] Jeanine Thweatt-Bates, *Cyborg Selves,* 6.

[54] Jeanine Thweatt-Bates, *Cyborg Selves,* 11.

[55] Cyborg is a feminist posthuman construction, birthed in the landmark essay "A Cyborg Manifesto" by Donna J. Haraway. The hybrid embodiment of the cyborg serves as a symbol for the ontological kinship of the human with the nonhuman. See Jeanine Thweatt-Bates, *Cyborg Selves,* 5.

[56] Scott A. Midson, *Cyborg Theology: Humans Technology and God* (London and New York: I.B. Tauris, 2018), 113.

are rooted in appeals to nature in substantive and discreet ways that suggest innocence."[57] So the premise of non-teleological cyborg is not understood as absolute, but helps in placing the discourse of reconfiguring the anthropology that helps in challenging the stumbling blocks in cyberspace.

Jeanine Thweat-Bates says,

> Haraway uses Cyborg as a critique of feminist essentialism. In which the identity of woman qua woman is assumed to be naturally given, self-evident and unchanging. She points out that challenging patriarchal and colonial essential tendencies eventually leads to the conclusion that all claims of identity based on a natural or organic point, is suspect. Identifying herself as a cyborg is Haraway's symbolic shorthand for the rejection of any attempt to define human identity on the basis of nature. This is crucial in the deliberate breakdown of the dichotomy between nature and technology which we can employ in the context of cyberspace.[58]

Bates credits Haraway as being non-teleological by contesting essentialism and discourse of nature. Technology and cyberspace has an imposing ethos and therefore the natural debate can be used to manipulate or subjugate other humans by people who are in power. Therefore, researcher understands that this approach has a subversive nature, which is important.

Midson states,

> In this understanding, close to Haraway's views on nature, the cyborg becomes a way to actively challenge what it is to be 'natural' in the first place. This is useful because notions of the 'natural' guide so many of our attitudes and practices. At present, our technological engagements are informed by notions of human nature as capable of changing the world for the better, or in need

[57] Scott A. Midson, *Cyborg Theology,* 113.

[58] Jeanine Thweatt-Bates, *Cyborg Selves,* 15.

> of augmenting, or in need of protecting and conserving against technological amendments. The cyborg scrutinises these assumptions about human nature.[59]

As Haraway would put it, "The cyborg is resolutely committed to partiality, irony, intimacy, and perversity. It is oppositional, utopian and completely without innocence. No longer structured by the polarity of public and private, the cyborg defines a technological polis based partly on a revolution of social relations in the *oikos,* the household."[60] Shah summarises that "Haraway's contributions to the imagination and formulation of cyborgs has been extraordinary, because not only did she dissolve the earlier mind-body, biology-technology divides but she also envisioned the cyborg as embodying a position of power and political resistance."[61]

Researcher finds this anthropology very appropriate as it does not negate technology, neither does it glorify it. It has an inherent mechanism to contest perfection portrayed either by technology or humanity as it contests any essentialism or dualisms. Non-Teleological framework helps in negating the techno-optimistic strand while counteracting technology as salvation. Non-Teleological strand interestingly helps to counteract all the possible arguments against technology by helping in balancing and engaging with it.

---

[59] Scott A. Midson, "The Cyborg and the Human: Origins, Creatureliness and Hybridity in Theological Anthropology" (Ph.D. dissertation, University of Manchester, 2015), 62.

It thereby allows us to critically reflect on the things that we value, those that we should value, and how we might connect the dots between the two. A useful starting point here is how the cyborg rejects notions of an independent or pre-existent nature that is defined against the technologised human who distances his/herself from the state of non-technological 'naturalness.'" One can identify three key strands to categorise and explore these theological (hi)stories that are most relevant to an understanding of both the cyborg and the human. They are: (1) origins; (2) creatureliness; and (3) hybridity. They are significant because the cyborg, articulated by Haraway, rejects discrete notions of humanness and human nature in favour of an emphasis on mixity and non-separation. In other words, for Haraway, "cyborg anthropology attempts to refigure provocatively the border relations among specific humans, other organisms, and machines."

[60] Donna Haraway, *Simians, Cyborgs, and Women*, 151.

[61] Nishant Shah, "The Technosocial Subject, 214.

1.4.2. Cyborg Anthropology

After the theoretical exposition of Non-Teleological Cyborg, the researcher wishes to see the practical ways in which Cyborg anthropology manifests in the context of cyberspace.

1.4.2.1. How do Humans Become Cyborgs?

Agnes Brazal says that Cyborg is an organism that improves its capacities through technology.[62] Hayles shows the fluid continuum of body and machine by saying, "Wherein no essential differences between bodily existence and computer simulation, cybernetic mechanism and biological organism, robot teleology and human goals, exist."[63] Brazal says, "We become cyborgs when our hands touches the mouse, when we use the smartphone and so on. In viewing the human as cyborg, the technology is no longer something one has uses/uses but becomes a part of one's self, a prosthesis or an artificial replacement of a body part (thus the reimaging of the human as half-human, half-machine)."[64] Donna Haraway notes, "The machines is us, our processes, an aspect of our embodiment."[65] Karen Vold states,

In 2014, the United States Supreme Court used this observation to justify the decision that police must obtain a warrant before rummaging through our smartphones. These devices 'are now

---

[62] Some would say that humans have been cyborgs ever since they started constructing tools to adapt to their environment. Today, however, especially because of cyberspace and micro-electronics revolution, the technology is no longer outside us but embedded within us (eg. Pacemaker) while communication technologies which are wireless and which we can carry with us everywhere. See Agnes M. Brazal, "A Cyborg Spirituality and Its Theo-Anthropological Foundation" in *Feminist Cyberethics in Asia: Religious Discourses in Connectivity*, edited by Agnes M. Brazal and Kochurani Abraham (New York: Palgrave Macmillan, 2014), 213.

[63] N. Katherine Hayles, *How We Became Posthuman: Virtual Bodies in Cybernetics, Literature, and Informatics* (Chicago and London: University of Chicago Press, 1999), 3.

[64] Agnes M. Brazal, "A Cyborg Spirituality and Its Theo-Anthropological Foundation" in *Feminist Cyberethics in Asia: Religious Discourses in Connectivity*, edited by Agnes M. Brazal and Kochurani Abraham (New York: Palgrave Macmillan, 2014), 200.

[65] Donna J. Haraway, *Simians, Cyborgs, and Women*, 180.

such a pervasive and insistent part of daily life that the proverbial visitor from Mars might conclude they were an important feature of human anatomy', as Chief Justice John Roberts observed in his written opinion. There is a wry observation that smartphones have become part of our body. If our minds now encompass our phones, we are essentially cyborgs: part-biology, part-technology.[66]

So, the fluidity of biology-technology makes one manifest the expression of humans as cyborgs, not as something of mechanical cyborg or ones seen in sci-fi movies, but as the anthropology of humans in the context of cyberspace.

1.4.2.2. Cyborg-Cyberspace Continuum

Understanding the cyborg-cyberspace continuum is central in the given search. David Hakken says,

> Generally attributed to William Gibson's novel Neuromancer (1984), "cyberspace" first referred to an electronic communication notional space. Essentially a collection of spatial metaphors, like the notion "desktop" employed in explanations of how to use an Apple Macintosh computer, cyberspace is now regularly used to refer collectively to computer-related social fields. The view of Robbie Davis-Floyd, for example, who asks us to consider whether, as we enter cyberspace, we wish to become more "cyborgic" and less "human." The notion that in cyberspace we do indeed become something so profoundly different that we cease to be persons in the normal sense is a common refrain or "trope" in cyberspace talk. Because they have always been technological and biological, and therefore cyborgic unities, I use "cyborg" to refer to all the entities that carry human culture.[67]

---

[66] Karina Vold, "Are 'you' just inside your skin or is your smartphone part of you?" *Aeon*, 26 February 2018, accessed 18 Nov. 2018, https://aeon.co/ideas/are-you-just-inside-your-skin-or-is-your-smartphone-part-of-you.

[67] David Hakken, *Cyborgs@Cyberspace? An Ethnographer Looks to the Future* (New York: Routledge, 1999), 5.

Therefore, it has become pronounced that the substantive or discreet identity of humans is a construct that stands contested. In cyberspace, humans as cyborg expresses the continuum of cyborg-cyberspace which gives fluidity in the further course of research.

1.4.2.3. Making of Cyborg in Cyberspace

The range of human-machine relationships has been diverse and varied. Haraway says, "We also live in Cyborg societies."[68] Nishant Shah reminds that "The spaces that we inhabit constantly remind us of the machinations that we are dependent on; sometimes using this to blind us of our dependence on the technology, sometimes to make it starkly visible. We deploy technologies that frame our daily survival at the flick of casual buttons and switches, clicks and thoughts."[69] He continues,

> The condition of cyborgification is peculiar; on the one hand, we have a biological body that enters into conditions of technologisation. However, this immersion in technologised conditions does not lead to the cyborgification. It simply provides a platform where the body is extended into different circuits, constructed as a database of objects that can be translated from one system to another imaged as a node within a network, recognised as an archive of several practices through which the extensions and digital representation are created. On the other hand, these imagined identities gain currency and have tactile and material consequences which are mapped on to the body of the cyborg. The cyborg, then, resides neither in the biological body nor in the digital representations, but in the practices by which these two separate, self-referencing, often overlapping entities are reconciled to exist, each mapped on to the other.[70]

---

[68] Donna Haraway, *Simians, Cyborgs, and Women,* 12.

[69] Nishant Shah, "The Technosocial Subject: Cities, Cyborgs and Cyberspace" (Ph.D. dissertation, Manipal University, 2012), 189.

[70] Nishant Shah, "The Technosocial Subject, 198-99.

The cyborfication is not a distinct or substantive identity, but constant interaction and practices which bring forth this hybrid identity which will help in understanding the changing anthropology or to comprehend cyborg anthropology that indicates hybridity.

1.4.2.4. Digital Cyborg

Social media is the digital realm that one needs to comprehend the phenomenon of humans becoming cyborg Nishant Shah observes, "Within cyberspaces, Social Networking Systems, Blogs, Multiple User Dungeons (MUD), Discussion Boards, Media sharing platforms, p2p networks,[71] etc., all create different conditions within which the physical users, through their digital avatars, interact with each other and form complex models of social networking and personal narratives."[72] Within Facebook and Instragam, the profile of the person is bound to the physical body of the user behind the profile. As William Mitchell points out in *Me ++* , "users in virtual worlds generally think of themselves as part of a larger database"[73] and also as "transmutable, transferable sets of data which they have authored for themselves - and can mobilise their virtual self across different networks to enhance their sense of social interaction and networking."[74] Shah continues,

> This dialectic offers an interesting approach to looking at the self-avatar relationship that is central to the discussions of Cyborg. On the one hand, it is the physical body of the user that produces the information which constitutes the digital self and presence, and hence it should be looked

[71] P2P Networks – Peer - to - Peer networks inherit the cyberspatial aesthetics of decentralized networks; of nodes being distributed across the circuits of the internet and talking to each other, collaborating in projects, sharing information, and exchanging digital material. The p2p networks have been the focus of scrutiny because they allow for unmonitored piracy and exchange of information. See Ankur Gupta, "Peer-To-Peer Networks and Computation: Current Trends and Future Perspectives" *Computing and Informatics* Vol. 30, (2011), 560.

[72] Nishant Shah, "The Technosocial Subject, 199.

[73] William Mitchell, *Me++: The Cyborg Self and the Network City*. (Cambridge: MIT Press, 1998), 45.

[74] William Mitchell, *Me++*, 56.

> upon as the primary or the authentic text. The avatar or profile is the point of contact and response and is greater than the information produced by the individual that the avatar is usually attributed to. The responses that the profile receives, the way in which the self is represented, are all the practices of the digital avatar.[75]

Clay Shirky observes that "The avatar is not constituted solely by the information or the text or persona produced by the physical user. In its very distributed-consolidated mode, it acquires and feeds off information of data streams that are outside of the control of the physical user."[76] Shah summarises,

> On Facebook and Instagram, the text and the pictures are not just the product of the self. It is built in negotiations with the users that gives rise to a different identity. This production of the meta-data introjects[77] the avatar into a circuit of meaning making and producing narratives that is beyond the scope of the physical body. This is a new context within which the avatar acquires value or reputation which is distinctly different from the reputation circuits that the biological body behind the avatar inhabits. The slippage between the avatar and the user is where the cyborg can be located. Neither the physical body nor the translated digital self. It resides in the interface between the two, each constantly referring to the other, creating an interminable loop of dependence. The cyborg, because it is produced by the very technologies of the two systems that it is straddling, makes these techniques or the technologisation of the self, synonymous with the processes of producing the narratives or making meaning. This is the digital cyborg.[78]

---

[75] Nishant Shah, "The Technosocial Subject, 201.

[76] Clay Shirky, *Here Comes Everybody: The Power of Organizing without Organizations.* (New York: Penguin, 2008), 53.

[77] to incorporate (attitudes or ideas) into one's personality unconsciously.

[78] Nishant Shah, "The Technosocial Subject, 205.

So, it becomes clear that the identity formed is neither of the biological entity nor of the profile avatar, but an interaction creates a hybrid identity which is known as the digital cyborg and this understanding is crucial in the research.

1.4.2.5. Embodied Cyborgs

Within the cyberspaces, as Sherry Turkle mentions, "the self gets created within screen worlds so that we experience reality as mediated by technology."[79] Kevin Warwick says,

> The cyborg is an individual who is not merely a node in the networked neighbourhood of interactive technologies but an organism that has internalized technology so that it becomes a part of its neuro-sensory circuits, thus producing an identity that more intelligently and effectively interacts with its immediate environment. Cyborg destabilises the human-machine divide or privilege and instead brings about a symbiotic relationship between the two.[80]

The non-invasive relation that a body produces by touching a keyboard or screen or gadget is beyond the individual capacities of each and this augments the body in cyberspaceto be known as embodied cyborg. Embodiment in the context is very critical and this therefore makes the anthropology theoretically sound and also helps to be realistic about the context which needs engagement. The factor of redemption of the context will come in the section of theological anthropology which will be seen in the next chapter.

1.5. Conclusion

Firstly, in this chapter, different strands of Posthuman discourse were surveyed. The researcher finds a lot of interesting insights in the Transhumanist discourse but the emphasis on disembodiment and a continuum of enlightenment paradigm that maintains a mind/

---

[79] Sherry Turkle, *Life on the Screen: Identity in the Age of the Internet* (New York: Touchstone Books, 1996), 3.

[80] Stephen Warwick, *I, Cyborg…*, 61.

body dualism and privileges the mind is dangerous a discourse on cyberspace and technology. The discourse does not offer any critique on cyberspace but has positivist affirmations which make the discourse lopsided and unhelpful to engage. Therefore, the researcher will not consider the strand of transhumanism in the further explorations.

Secondly, one has observed the discourse on cyborg as the other strand under postfoundationalism. Cyborg is not a monolithic discourse but the researcher has not included a gamut of strands as it would be beyond the scope of the research. The researcher has expounded on the understanding of cyborg as and how it would be meaningful in the research.

Thirdly, the researcher finds the non-teleological discourse of cyborg espoused by Donna Haraway, the most useful to represent the context of cyberspace in the Posthuman discourse. The essential understanding of human based on substance understanding privileges humans and makes any dialogue with technology or cyberspace next to impossible. This discourse counters all essential understanding of natural that idealizes a primal state or Eden. The dichotomy between the natural/technology/cyberspace is held in tension without giving a sacred sanction to those considered natural. Also this strand takes embodiment and materiality very seriously which is fundamental in our dialogue. Therefore, this strand will be used as cyborg in the future usage of research to symbolize and engage, in the context of cyberspace.

Chapter 2

Exploring the Landscape of Theological Anthropology

Introduction

The question of "Who am I?" is seen as a central quest of human life. But, this search is not in a void. The identity of human beings are viewed in relationship with origins like a creator and in relationship with the context with other human beings along with the creation, artifacts like infrastructure and technology and all that contribute to the process of living. Apart from God, a human primacy is assumed which has come under criticism, may it be regarding ecology or in dialogue with science and technology. As seen in the earlier discourse of posthumanism, there is a clear decentering of human beings. Therefore, this chapter would understand the premise of theological anthropology and survey different typologies of *Imago Dei*, so as to find a dialogical partner with the cyborg as surveyed in the previous chapter.

2.1. Theological Anthropology: A Definition

It is important to understand a clear premise of theological anthropology. Nungshitula, a Naga Theologian says "Theological Anthropology defines a human being in relation to God, fellow human beings, non-human beings and the whole of the cosmos. It is the study and destiny of human beings, their standing in front of the creator and their task ahead."[81] "It also investigates the inter-relatedness of human beings with the creation and the human-made ethos where theological anthropology does not reject anything, rather it values everything as all are parts of the web of life."[82] David H. Kesley gives us a more precise definition where he says "Theological Anthropology is doctrine about human nature or what is to be a person."[83] Burns gives the discipline a sense of location and direction, "It investigates the resources, the limitations and the destiny of the human person."[84] Distinctive features of Theological Anthropology are as follows.

2.1.1. Varied Understandings in Theological Anthropology

Theological Anthropology is also defined as to include ways in which human beings are related to each other and rest of God's creation. S. J Samartha states,

> It is time not just to solidify the special status of the human being, but to look for ways to live as human beings in the global community, where the emphasis on uniqueness or separateness has to give way to togetherness to recover a sense of wholeness, a sacred and mysterious

---

[81] Nungshitula, *The Naga Images of Human Being: A Resource for Contemporary Theological Anthropology* (Jorhat: Tribal Study Centre, 2001), 16.

[82] Nungshitula, *The Naga Images of Human Being,* 16.

[83] David H. Kesley, "Human Being" in *Christian Theology: An Introduction to its Traditions and Tasks,* edited by Peter C. Hodgson and Robert H. King (Philadelphia: Fortress Press, 1986), 167.

[84] J. Patout Burns, *Theological Anthropology* (Philadelphia: Fortress Press, 1981), 1.

> space, within which nature, humanity and God are held together within a differentiated unity.[85]

Theological Anthropology will make sense only in the paradigm of a human being, called Jesus Christ. Kesley notes "As a paradigm of what personhood ought to be, it is replaced by the story of Jesus who is at once the truly actualized person and the image of God."[86] "Jesus Christ is the central reference that makes the existence of human beings and the rest of creation meaningful is the incarnation, historical life of Jesus, crucifixion and resurrection as all is contained in person of Jesus-God become human"[87] adds Jose Comblin.

Van Huyststeen notes that:

> The Christian tradition offers a rich, historical diversity of interpretation of the question, "What does it mean to be human?" At the center of Christian theological anthropology is the depiction of the creation of humankind in the image of God. Despite its importance and centrality, *Imago Dei* remains ambiguous, prompting a long history of theological interpretation of the primary and yet stubbornly mysterious aspect of human being.[88]

In the light of above points, the observations show that there is no neat accepted understanding of Theological Anthropology, as there are multiple voices. The centrality of *Imago Dei* is established but is not as obvious as assumed. The researcher will try a brief overview of the Biblical texts referring to the *Imago Dei*. This will be followed by a discussion of three major typologies of *Imago Dei* within the Christian tradition. Van Huyssteen observes, "The central

---

[85] S. J. Samartha, "Images of the Human: A Search for Wholeness," in *Asian Journal of Theology*, Vol. 8, No. 2. (October 1994), 261.

[86] David H. Kesley, "Human Being," 182.

[87] Jose Comblin, *Retreiving the Human: A Christian Anthropology* (Maryknoll: Orbis Books, 1990), 222.

[88] J. Wentzel van Huyssteen, *Alone in the World? Human Uniqueness in Science and Theology*, The Glifford Lectures (Grand Rapids, MI, 2006), 313-14.

theological notion of the *Imago Dei* exists within the Christian tradition as a set of complex theological mini-theories rather than as a univocal concept."[89] This does not dilute the importance of the concept, but helps in understanding how contested and negotiable the concept is.

2.1.2. Fluid Images of God

There is no uniform understanding of *Imago Dei.* Noreen Herzfeld used three passages from Genesis 1:26-28, 5:3 and 9:6 to elucidate the concept of Image of God. She says, "There are two observations regarding Genesis 1:26-28: first, that the creation of human beings in God's image is connected to the phrase 'male and female,' and second, that the image is twice connected to the idea of dominion over the other animals."[90] She continues "Genesis 5:3 connects the creation of humankind in God's likeness to Adam's fathering of a son, Seth, in Adam's likeness; which indicates that the divine image is inherited by Seth, and that the image is transmitted from parent to child."[91]

> Genesis 9:6 connects the divine image with the ethical prohibition against murder, within the context of giving human beings permission to kill and eat the flesh of other animals and therefore one can conclude from this passage: 1) All human beings participate in the Image of God, regardless of gender or generation, 2) only human beings are created in this image, thus they are distinguished from nonhuman animals, and 3) human life is to be valued because of God's image.[92]

---

[89] J. Wentzel van Huyssteen, *Alone in the World,* 314.

[90] Noreen Herzfeld, *In Our Image: Artificial Intelligence and the Human Spirit* (Minneapolis: Fortress Press, 2002), 11-12.

[91] Noreen Herzfeld, *In Our Image: Artificial Intelligence and the Human Spirit,* 12.

[92] Noreen Herzfeld, *In Our Image: Artificial Intelligence and the Human Spirit,* 13.

Bates summarizes that "First can be labelled as the Universality of the *Imago Dei*, second emphasizes the ontological uniqueness of humans while the third highlights the moral status of the *Imago Dei* in humanity."[93] J. Wentzel van Huyssteen adds another Genesis passage to the three above, Genesis 3:22 in which Adam and Eve become like God,[94] in possessing the knowledge of good and evil which calls for epistemological likeness.[95]

New Testament references of *Imago Dei,* add an important Christian dimension to the concept in interpreting Jesus the Christ as paradigmatic and the true image of God. Stanley J. Grenz says, "This not only establishes Christ as a mediating figure between humanity and divinity, but introduces a progressive, moral dimension to the Image of God in that becoming 'Christ-like' means perfecting the Image of God within ourselves to better conformity with the true image revealed in Jesus Christ."[96] As seen above, *Imago Dei* is not something consistently found in the Bible, but it has been very important as it emphasizes the universal, ontological, moral and epistemological uniqueness of humans. Jesus Christ as the true *Imago Dei,* brings the disclosure to its climax.

2.2. Typologies of *Imago Dei*

Herzfeld helps in understanding that the Scriptural references of Image of God is an important theological content but none are prescriptive of the image.[97] This leads to three typologies of *Imago Dei*

---

[93] Jeanine Thweatt-Bates, *Cyborg Selves: A Theological Anthropology of the Posthuman, 110.*

[94] So this calls for an epistemological likeness, an albeit problematic one, as the passage describes "the fall" of humankind into sin. Van Huyssteen says that "The epistemological dimension of *Imago Dei* questions the presumed boundary between human and divine: the ultimate focus on this thin line between the divine and the human worlds finally culminates in breaking down of the necessary boundaries between these two worlds." See J. Wentzel van Huyssteen, *Alone in the World,* 123.

[95] J. Wentzel van Huyssteen, *Alone in the World,* 123.

[96] Stanley J Grenz, "Jesus As The *Imago Dei*: Image-of-God Christology and the Non-Linear Linearity of Theology" in *Journal of Evangelical Society 47/4* (December 2004), 618-19.

[97] Noreen Herzfeld, *In Our Image,* 13.

that can be grouped as substantive, functional and relational.[98] The researcher, as explained in the introduction, will choose functional typology but the other two will be brought into debate to make the search more comprehensive.

2.2.1. Functional Typology

The functional typology of the *Imago Dei* finds its expression in the agency of human being. Karl Barth observes, "It is the human function itself that is created in the image of God. This view has been around since at least the times of the Ancient Near East where their ontology was functional and was a weaker image of mythological gods whose identities were also purely functional."[99] Herzfeld articulates that "Johannes Hehn was the first to introduce a non-substantive interpretation in his 1915 article *Zum Terminus Bild Gottes* based on extra-biblical sources. Hehn defined the Image of God as a royal kingship rather than as a quality intrinsic to human nature."[100] Herzfeld builds on

> Old Testament scholar Gerhard von Rad and many other scholars modified Hehn's work into a functional view of *Imago Dei* based on biblical exegesis. Von Rad argued that the only clear evidence for the concept in Genesis 1 is that human beings are created in the Image of God so that they may have dominion over the entire creation. Thus, for him, the *Imago Dei* signifies the function of humanity.[101]

Eugene H. Merrill explains this as the creation mandate, in which humanity is given a clear responsibility of multiplying on the earth and having dominion over all creation (Gen 1:26-27; Gen 2:18-20). He rightly states that humankind as both male and

---

[98] Millard J. Erickson, *Christian Theology* (Grand Rapids: Baker Book House, 1985), 95.

[99] Karl Barth, "The Covenant as the Internal Basis of Creation," In *Church Dogmatics*, Vol. III/1 (Peabody, MA: Hendrickson Publishers, 2010), 207.

[100] Noreen Herzfeld, *In Our Image*, 20.

[101] Noreen Herzfeld, *In Our Image*, 20-21.

female, functions as the Image of God (Gen 1:28).[102] Merrill reports an alternative argument of the meaning of the *Imago Dei* which is based on grammatical evidence.[103] Accordingly, there are scholars who argue that humanity is not in the image showing substance, but is the Image of God, showing functionality. This means, according to Merrill, that "Humanity does not so much share with God his essential reality, but rather, is a representative of that reality. That is, humankind has a functional role to play, a role that requires no ontological commonness with God."[104] Merrill concludes that combining both the grammatical and the intra-textual evidence helps to highlight the full significance of the *Imago Dei* as he claims, "Humankind is in the Image of God but also serves as the image. Humans have resemblance to God, even if limited, but stand in God's place in the administration of God's creation."[105] Gerhard von Rad argued in favor of translating the Hebrew *bĕṣelem ʾĕlœhîm* as "as the image of God," based on which he not only rejects the interpretation that limits God's image to man's spiritual nature but also articulates that "the whole man physical and spiritual is created in God's image."[106] Midson gives a sharper summing up as "There need be no trait in God after which some quality of human was patterned. Rather, human beings image God when they function in God's stead, as God's representative on earth."[107] So, the representation and functionality is focused upon, rather than being patterned by the original creative act of God. This gives freedom to humans which is important in the debate.

Researcher understands that functional interpretation does not endow human beings with divine essence. Midson notes, "Functional accounts of theological anthropology thereby provide a

[102] Eugene H. Merrill, "Image of God," in *Dictionary of the Old Testament: Pentateuch*, edited by T. Desmond Alexander and David W. Baker (Downers Grove, IL: InterVarsity Press, 2003), 442-443.

[103] Eugene H. Merrill, "Image of God," 443.

[104] Eugene H. Merrill, "Image of God," 443.

[105] Eugene H. Merrill, "Image of God," 443-444.

[106] Gerhard Von Rad, *Genesis: A Commentary* (Philadelphia, PA: The Westminister Press, 1972), 58.

[107] Noreen Herzfeld, *In Our Image,* 20-21.

way of grounding ethical judgments on human activity in the world, rather than being concerned with abstract, static qualities."[108] So the matrix of the context is the reference point to judge the human functionality rather than the recreation of an ideal, which is perfect, invisible and abstract. The point where the functional interpretation of *Imago Dei* becomes more significant is when it is read in the context of a techno-cultural milieu. Philip Hefner says, "To be created in the Image of God implies that humans can be the vehicle for grace toward the creation, in a way that is somehow reminiscent of God's graciousness."[109] Brain Brock says, "Technologies problematise our ability to rely on an originary set of ethics because of how it transforms, to various degrees depending on the technology in question, the environment around it."[110] So in regards to technology, should one disregard origins? Midson disagrees, "We rely on mythical-theological assumptions to make assessments of ourselves and nonhuman others. Many technologies are actually produced out of these assumptions and worldviews."[111] So, the origins is important in functional typology unlike its cyborg anthropology, but origin does not dictate to be replicated but is seen as a guidance or being in continuation. The functional typology also emphasizes about creative capacity, but there is an openness as pointed by Midson, which is the dimension of freedom in a technological milieu like cyberspace.[112]

Researcher finds the concerned typology best suited for the context as the representational character of functional typology does not assume essential oneness with God. This typology emphasizes that the *Imago Dei* is endowed in the whole body and personhood of human being. Crucial advantage of this typology is that it highlights humans as creative agents.

---

[108] Scott A. Midson, *Cyborg Theology*, 33.

[109] Philip Hefner, *The Human Factor: Evolution, Culture and Religion* (Minneapolis: Fortress Press, 1993), 238

[110] Brian Brock, *Christian Ethics in a Technological Age* (Michigan: Eerdmans Publishing Company, 2010), 2.

[111] Scott A. Midson, *Cyborg Theology*, 34.

[112] Scott A. Midson, "The Cyborg and the Human, 125.

2.2.2. Choosing an *Imago Dei* Motif under Functional Typology

In continuation with the above premise, there are three aspects that the researcher wishes to choose for functional typology to choose an appropriate metaphor. Marc Cortez line of argument is that functional typology has 3 aspects, i.e., dominion, creativity and imitation.[113]

Firstly, dominion is a contested concept and therefore one strand of thought as Vice-Regent will be used. Cortez quotes John Bolt saying, "that humans were created for "creative production.""[114] Cortez quotes Bolt again to define creative production as "using the manifold riches of creation to enhance human flourishing."[115] As there is a danger of exclusionary tendency in Vice-Regent, Bolt again helps where he states "being an image bearer is a status bestowed by God."[116] This could be understood as a gift than a status as Bolt says "In a Christian worldview, being precedes doing."[117] Further, Bolt says that image "is properly oriented towards what Christ will do."[118] So, the Christological element is critical in being a Vice-Regent which Cortez says is revealed to be a Created Co-Creator.[119] Therefore, the connection of Dominion or Vice-regent is seen in Created Co-Creator.

Secondly, Cortez quotes Dorothy Sayers to say that *Imago Dei* is about creativity.[120] Cortez says,

> Work is a way of life in which the nature of man should find its proper exercise and delight and so fulfill itself to

---

[113] Marc Cortez, "Vocationalizing the *Imago Dei,*" accessed 25 Jan. 2019, https://www.wheaton.edu/media/opus/Cortez–Vocationalizing-the-imago-Dei.pdf.

[114] John Bolt, *Economic Shalom: A Reformed Primer on Faith, Work and Human Flourishing* (Michigan: Christian's Library Press, 2013), 28.

[115] Marc Cotez, "Vocationalizing the *Imago Dei,*" accessed 25 Jan. 2019.

[116] John Bolt, *Economic Shalom,* 29.

[117] John Bolt, *Economic Shalom,* 38.

[118] John Bolt, *Economic Shalom,* 29.

[119] Marc Cotez, "Vocationalizing the *Imago Dei.*"

[120] Marc Cotez, "Vocationalizing the *Imago Dei.*"

> the glory of God. That it should, in fact, be thought of as a creative activity undertaken for the love of the work itself; and that man, made in God's image, should make things, as God makes them, for the sake of doing well a thing that is well worth doing.[121]

Here again one can see the implication of vocation and the vision as Created Co-Creator.

Thirdly, Cortez quoting Wayne Grudum talks of *Imago Dei* as imitation in the functional view.[122] Grudum talks about *Imago Dei* as the "imitation of the attributes of God."[123]

In cognizance with the above parameters, Philip Hefner's CCC deems to be the most appropriate metaphor to engage with the cyborg anthropology. Stephen Garner opines that "A functional approach to the *Imago Dei*, mediated through the metaphor of co-creation, goes a significant way towards explaining human beings proclivity for technology and the desire to transform themselves and the world. It creates a framework to answer some of the ontological questions about who and what human beings are within technoculture."[124] The elaboration of Created Co-Creator will be done in the next chapter along with the methodology to engage with. Researcher will engage the debate of substantive typology which has been the most prominent debate in theological anthropology. The relational typology has been recent, but will enrich in the larger understanding of the subject and expand the horizon of the research.

2.2.3. Substantive Typology

Since one has chosen Functional Typology, the other typologies does not become irrelevant. Even the reason for not selecting it

---

[121] Marc Cotez, "Vocationalizing the *Imago Dei*."

[122] Marc Cotez, "Vocationalizing the *Imago Dei*."

[123] Wayne Grudum, *Business For the Glory of God: The Bible's Teachings on the Moral Goodness of Business* (Illinois: Crossway Books, 2003), 13.

[124] Stephen Garner, "Living in the Borderlands: Cyborgs and the *Imago Dei*," accessed 25 Jan. 2019, https://www.researchgate.net/publication/242247017_Living_in_the_Borderlands_Cyborgs_and_the_Imago_Dei.

will further the given debate. One of the earliest and arguably most pervasive interpretations of *Imago Dei* is known as the substantive interpretation. Lewis and Demarest defines, "The substantive view maintains that the *Imago Dei* exists formally as a God-like attribute within the composition of the human."[125] Burns points out that "Irenaeus (A.D. 130-c. 202) saw a distinction between the "image" and the "likeness" of God. He defined the "image" as the endowments of reason and will that were intact after the 'Fall'. He defined "likeness" as the life of the spirit that was lost after the 'Fall,' but could become regenerated by grace."[126] Of the different substantive interpretations researcher finds the 'likeness' aspect of Irenaeus very sound and worth considering in the further debate. Leron Shults points that "Substance[127] orientation is there due to the influence of Platonic and Aristotelian philosophical categories on the early formation and articulation of Theological Anthropology."[128] Substance dualism has influenced the concept of *imago dei.* Aleazar Fernandez uses this as a premise to find out that "The guiding questions to be asked was,

---

[125] Gordon R. Lewis and Bruce A. Demarest, *Integrative Theology,* Vol. 2 (Grand Rapids, MI: Zondervan, 1996), 126.

[126] J. Patout Burns, *Theological Anthropology*, 27.

[127] There are two ways of talking about philosophical concept of *substance.* For theis research, only the first one is relevant, therefore we will consider only that which is more generic. The philosophical term 'substance' corresponds to the Greek *ousia*, which means 'being,' transmitted via the Latin *substantia*, which means 'something that stands under or grounds things'. According to the generic sense, therefore, the substances in a given philosophical system are those things which, according to that system, are the foundational or fundamental entities of reality. Thus, for an atomist, atoms are the substances, for they are the basic things from which everything is constructed. In David Hume's system, impressions and ideas are the substances, for the same reason. In a slightly different way, Forms are Plato's substances, for everything derives its existence from Forms. In this sense of 'substance' any realist philosophical system acknowledges the existence of substances. Probably the only theories which do not would be those forms of logical positivism or pragmatism which treat ontology as a matter of convention. According to such theories, there are no real facts about what is ontologically basic, and so nothing is objectively substance. See "Substance," in *Stanford Encyclopedia of Philosophy,* accessed on 13 Nov. 2018, https://plato.stanford.edu/entries/substance/.

[128] F. LeRon Shults, *Reforming Theological Anthropology: After Philosophical Turn to Relationality* (Grand Rapids: Abingdon Press, 2003), 167.

therefore, how the substance of the soul and the substance of the body were related, such that they constituted one's personal identity, and, what were the faculties of the soul, and how did they relate to each other and to the body?"[129] Shults shows that substantive interpretations of *Imago Dei,* whether classical or contemporary, lead to the anthropological constructions that privilege disembodied notions of intellect, rationality, mind or soul as an essential aspect of human nature where Augustine of Hippo adopted a Neoplatonic[130] anthropology in which the soul and the body were distinguished as separate substances, and identified the self with the substance of the soul rather than the body.[131] Augustine identifies the soul as a

---

[129] Eleazar S. Fernandez, *Reimagining the Human: Theological Anthropology in Response to Systemic Evil* (Missouri: Chalice Press, 2004), 17.

[130] The term "Neoplatonism" refers to a philosophical school of thought that first emerged and flourished in the Greco-Roman world of late antiquity, roughly from the time of the Roman Imperial Crisis to the Arab conquest, i.e., the middle of the 3rd to the middle of the 7th century. In consequence of the demise of ancient materialist or corporealist thought such as Epicureanism and Stoicism, Neoplatonism became the dominant philosophical ideology of the period, offering a comprehensive understanding of the universe and the individual human being's place in it. However, in contrast to labels such as "Stoic", "Peripatetic" or "Platonic", the designation "Neoplatonic" is of modern coinage. The most fundamental of these assumptions, which the Neoplatonists shared with the majority of intellectuals of the ancient world, including most pre-Socratic thinkers as well as Socrates, Plato, Aristotle and their followers, is that mindful consciousness (*nous*, often translated as thought, intelligence, or intellect) is in an important sense ontologically prior to the physical realm typically taken for ultimate reality (Mind over Matter). The second assumption, which the Neoplatonists shared with the Stoics and the Hermetists (an influential group of Egyptian religious thinkers that predate the rise of Neoplatonism), was that reality, in all its cognitive and physical manifestations, depended on a highest principle which is unitary and singular. Neoplatonic philosophy is a strict form of principle-monism that strives to understand everything on the basis of a single cause that they considered divine, and indiscriminately referred to as "the First", "the One", or "the Good." See "Neoplatonism," in *Stanford Encyclopedia of Philosophy,* accessed 13 Nov. 2018, https://plato.stanford.edu/entries/neoplatonism/.

[131] F. LeRon Shults, *Reforming Theological Anthropology,* 167-68.

certain substance, sharing in reason and suited to the task of ruling the body.[132] Bates succinctly points that:

> This line of thought was maintained by Thomas Aquinas in the *Summa Theologica*. Adopting Aristotle's hylomorphism,[133] Aquinas identifies the soul as the form of human being, and body as the matter, an anthropological construction less obviously dualistic

[132] Augustine of Hippo, *Greatness of the Soul: The Teacher,* Translated by Joseph M. Colleran (New York: The Newman Press, 1950), 18.

[133] Hylomorphism, (from Greek *hylē,* "matter"; *morphē,* "form"), in philosophy, w according to which every natural body consists of two intrinsic principles, one potential, namely, primary matter, and one actual, namely, substantial form. It was the central doctrine of Aristotle's philosophy of nature. Before Aristotle, the Ionian philosophers had sought the basic constituents of bodies; but Aristotle observed that it was necessary to distinguish two types of principles. On the one hand, one must look for the primordial elements—i.e., for bodies that are not derived from others and of which all other bodies are composed. He found his solution to this question in Empedocles' doctrine of the four elements: earth, water, air, and fire. On the other hand, one must look for the intrinsic conditions whereby a body is or comes to be what it is understood to be, and to answer this question he proposed his hylomorphic doctrine. The primordial elements correspond in a sense to those of modern physics insofar as the single elements can have independent existence or activity of their own and can therefore be known directly by way of experiment. Matter and form, however, are not bodies or physical entities that can exist or act independently: they exist and act only within and by the composite. Thus, they can be known only indirectly, by intellectual analysis, as the metaphysical principles of bodies. Aristotle based his argument chiefly on the analysis of "becoming," or substantial change. If a being changes into another being, something permanent must exist that is common to the two terms; otherwise there would be no transformation but merely a succession by the annihilation of the first term and the creation of the second. This permanent and common something cannot itself be strictly a being because a being already is and does not become, and because a being "in act" cannot be an intrinsic part of a being possessing a unity of its own; it must therefore be a being "in potency," a potential principle, passive and indeterminate. At the same time, in the two terms of the change, there must also be an actual, active, determining principle. The potential principle is matter, the actual principle, form. Phenomenological arguments for hylomorphism have also been proposed. The hylomorphic doctrine was received and variously interpreted by the Greek and Arab commentators of Aristotle and by the Scholastic philosophers. See "Hylomorphism," *Encyclopedia Britannica,* accessed 13 Nov. 2018, https://www.britannica.com/topic/hylomorphism.

> than the Platonic dualism of identifying body and soul as distinct substances.[134]

Robert Pasnua highlights that "when it comes to explaining the human mind (intellect and will), Aquinas has special reason for ignoring the body, inasmuch as he believes that these capacities of the soul are entirely immaterial."[135] Consequently, substantive typology[136] does help in understanding the uniqueness of human beings which is important. But, in the name of uniqueness, substantive typology highlights the supremacy of human beings which is a stumbling block to the research. This typology also assumes that humans share the essence of God which consequently denies the agency of human beings and restricts them be subordinate to the creative acts of God. This leaves a lot of interpretative power to the faith community which makes technology and innovation a subject of anxiety and apprehension. The context is consistently seen as sinful and corrupt and the positioning of the debate is a top-down approach. The researcher understands that such substantive interpretation of human beings has been a stumbling block in engaging a dialogue with science and technology, as the hierarchical interpretation privileges the humans which makes any association with rest of the creation or technological milieu as impossible with too much power wrested with humans who advocate the discourse. Substantive typology also values disembodied and abstract over embodied and specific. There are some minute strands of substantive that is useful. Substantive interpretation helped in understanding the conventional stumbling blocks that still remains a challenge to the discourse summed up in concepts like nature, essence, purity and substance which will be further discussed in the next chapter in the section of hybridity.

---

[134] Jeanine Thweatt-Bates, *Cyborg Selves,* 112.

[135] Robert Pasnau, *Thomas Aquinas On Human Nature* (Cambridge: Cambridge University Press, 2002), 32.

[136] David Fergusson emphasizes that "In theological anthropology, while substantive accounts of *Imago Dei* certainly remain valid alongside the human, animal and machine commonalities where *Imago Dei* does not enable some short cut to identifying a single property or function that differentiates us from other animals or machines." See David Fergusson, 'Humans Created according to the *Imago Dei*: An Alternative Proposal,' *Zygon* Vol. 48, No. 2 (2013), 449.

2.2.4. Relational Typology

Researcher understands that the relational aspect was always important in theology but the postmodern hermeneutics has emphasized its centrality. Lewis and Demarest observe that:

> When it comes to the relational aspect of *Imago Dei*, it seems that most theologians, even though they have not explicitly addressed the issue, have assumed that the relationship aspect somehow pertains to the Image of God, or at least leads to a discussion about the image of God. Yet, there is a group of theologians who put the relationship aspect at the very center of their understanding of what *Imago Dei* is or should be.[137]

F. LeRon Shults argues that,

> A philosophical 'turn to relationality' has reframed the contemporary theological task, and many theologians have rearticulated core theological and anthropological insights in the Christian tradition to reflect this. Though relationality is not a new concept for theology, the reciprocity between theological concepts and the philosophical and scientific ideas has obscured the nature and importance of relationality in the formation of Christian doctrine. The current emphasis on relationality is the philosophical turn to relationality which has its impact.[138]

Shults poignantly shows that "Aristotle was ascribed the substance understanding which dominated the western philosophical tradition which saw emergence of Kant and Hegel as turning points reorienting philosophical concepts away from categories of substance to categories of relations."[139] Shults stark

---

[137] Gordon R. Lewis and Bruce A. Demarest. *Integrative Theology. Three Volumes in One* (Grand Rapids, MI: Zondervan, 1996), 130-31.

[138] F. LeRon Shults, *Reforming Theological Anthropology: After the Philosophical Turn to Relationality* (Michigan: Wm. B. Eerdmans Publishing Co, 2003), 11.

[139] F. LeRon Shults, *Reforming Theological Anthropology*, 13.

criticism that the ontological categories of substance that informed the Christian traditions early grappling with anthropological and Christological identity shaped the interpretation of doctrine into forms that no longer make sense after the philosophical turn to relationality. Shults further opines,

> Therefore, it is contended that substance metaphysics, as a specific contextual influence on the formation of early Christian doctrine, can and should in some instances be discarded, and that the turn to relationality offers a new opportunity for presenting a Christian understanding of humanity in a way that upholds some key biblical intuitions that have sometimes been obscured or lost.[140]

Herzfeld refers to Karl Barth as the most influential advocate of relational interpretation of *Imago Dei*, who argued that the Image of God consists neither in human nature nor in their action, but is identified with the fact that humanity is a "counterpart to God."[141] She tells,

> For Barth, it is the "I-You" confrontation existing within the Trinity that lays a foundation for the divine-human and human-human relationship. Thus, the *Imago Dei* exists in the relationship[142] rather than in human capacity. Barth understands the image as having two meanings: God lives in togetherness with Himself, then God lives in togetherness with man, then men live in togetherness with one another.[143]

Anna Case-Winters sharpens the debate by saying "Enhanced rational and relational capacities do not need to be perceived as

---

[140] F. LeRon Shults, *Reforming Theological Anthropology,* 5.

[141] Noreen Herzfeld, *In Our Image,* 24.

[142] Barth means that we must recognize the other as both distinct from ourselves and as our true fellow. When we treat another as an extension of ourselves, when we withhold or conceal our inner being and do not let the other know us, we do not participate in full humanity. See Noreen Herzfeld, *In Our Image,* 25-26.

[143] Noreen Herzfeld, *In Our Image,* 25-26.

separating us from the rest of nature in some qualitatively different sense. These capacities admit of a more and a less, a continuum of gradations."[144] Anna Case-Winters further notes, "human beings, like every other reality, are co-constituted by their relationships. Relationships are internal."[145] S. Goizueta's contests human autonomy and individuality by emphasizing, "The human person is always intrinsically relational."[146] He says that "Humans are both biological and anthropological, as the individual is quite literally, given birth by and through the parents' relationship to each other and the new born."[147] Bates says that one is not talking of social dimensions of personhood alone, but also of human embodiment that makes a person, sacramental.[148]

Midson makes an important point by saying,

> The notion that humans, as well as other species, are formed by their relations means that attention needs to be distributed across all relating actors, and parties, rather than reducing the 'other' to a mere object against which the subject is dialectically defined. So, this makes it clear that no abstract concepts are there in relationship across networks. A relational interpretation has the merit of uncovering the plasticity of difference, as something contingent upon connections, still does not do anything to overcome that difference.[149]

Researcher agrees that relational interpretation gives a different lens in engaging the space of negotiation, where identities are formed in negotiation. It also helps in overcoming many challenges that are assumed in a technological milieu. By the understanding

---

[144] Anna Case-Winters, 'Rethinking the Image of God,' Zygon, Vol. 39, No. 4 (2004), 818.

[145] Anna Case-Winters, 'Rethinking the Image of God,' 818.

[146] Roberto S. Goizueta, *Caminemos Con Jesus: Toward a Hispanic/Latino Theology of Accompaniment* (New York: Orbis Books, 1995), 59.

[147] Roberto S. Goizueta, *Caminemos Con Jesus,* 59.

[148] Jeanine Thweatt-Bates, *Cyborg Selves,* 117.

[149] Scott A. Midson, *Cyborg Theology*, 40.

of relational typology of *Imago Dei,* researcher fears are too closely linked to the context unlike the functional which maintains a good distinction with God and context. Despite the merits, researcher quoting Scott Midson in the earlier statement understands that this interpretation helps to engage and understand the different identities that are divine, human, animal, machine, etc., and keeps the identity in relationality in a given context, but the redemption dimension is inadequate or missing. That is, relationality would make us subject to the context without any scope of transcending it.

2.3. Christology as the Lens for Theological Anthropology

The researcher has surveyed various options in the *Imago Dei* along with its typologies. In search of an authentic Christian formation, one cannot miss out on Christology that leads to this desired formation.

WCC document elaborates, "A Christian understanding of what it is to be human unfolds through shared engagement and mediation in the community of faith. A fuller account of who and what we are as humans emerges from the Church's prayerful engagement with each of these realms, as we keep the person of Jesus in focus."[150] This further says that Jesus is "the true image… of our humanity,"[151] we will understand "what we are as humans" if we "keep the person of Jesus in focus."[152] This is the "Christ-centred lens" through which we must look if we want to see what it really means to be human.[153] Consequently, the Christian understanding of true humanity is rooted in reflection on the person of Jesus Christ.[154] David Kesley claims that Christians understanding of theological

---

[150] World Council of Churches, *Christian Perspectives on Theological Anthropology: A Faith and Order Paper, No.199* (Geneva: World Council of Churches, 2005), 51.

[151] World Council of Churches, *Christian Perspectives on Theological Anthropology,* 33.

[152] World Council of Churches, *Christian Perspectives on Theological Anthropology,* 34.

[153] World Council of Churches, *Christian Perspectives on Theological Anthropology,* 36.

[154] World Council of Churches, *Christian Perspectives on Theological Anthropology,* 37.

anthropological issues "is shaped in some way by their beliefs about Jesus Christ and God's relation to him and that this is ultimately what qualifies theological answers to proposed anthropological questions as authentically Christian theological anthropology."[155] Researcher is of the opinion that theological anthropology, along with Christology will help in the search for formation as Christology is vital for the question of formation.

2.4. Conclusion

The researcher reviewed the landscape of theological anthropology and problematized that it does not have a univocal definition, but has pluriform voice. The strand of *Imago Dei* was seen important in theological anthropology and again, this too has various connotations and interpretations.

Primacy of human beings has been a stumbling block for a dialogical engagement with Science and Technology. The substantive interpretation was found emphasizing essence of humans and their primacy and therefore least useful in the research. In the analysis, the relational typology seems the most attractive. It surely helps in removing the stumbling blocks and makes the field dialogical, but the researcher has reasons that makes the relational typology good for understanding humans in a given context but does not help to redeem the context.

Functional typology debunks the essence and also reiterates ethics, and sees human beings as a representation which gives one a handle in engaging in a dialogue with technology. In the realm of functional typology, Philip Hefner's created Co-Creator typology will be used. The researcher understands Christology as integral in giving shape to the human formation. Christology reveals the true *Imago Dei* that will lead to authentic Christian human formation.

---

[155] David H. Kesley, *Eccentric Existence: A Theological Anthropology* (Louisville: Westminister John Knox, 2009), 8-9.

Chapter 3

Hybridity
Cyborg and Created Co-Creator as Dialogical Partners

Introduction

In Chapter one, the researcher explored the various Posthuman discourses to engage with cyberspace. Of the different strands, the researcher found the non-teleological cyborg and its philosophical grounds suitable for an anthropology of cyberspace. In Chapter two, the researcher surveyed various understandings of *Imago Dei* and of the various options, Functional typology was seen as most suitable. Philip Hefner's Created Co-Creator (CCC) was considered the most appropriate in this regard which will be explored later in the chapter. Cyborg is a hybrid concept. Hybridity as a methodology will be explored to engage with the ongoing conversations. Hybridity after being explored will delve into cyborg as hybrid. The importance of the proposal of CCC and how it is a hybrid concept will be explored in this chapter.

3.1. Hybridity as Methodology

The methodology of hybridity helps in integrating the various strands of the debate. Scott A. Midson in his Ph.D. dissertation[156] investigates and employs hybridity that has helped the researcher consider it as a methodology. The semantics of 'hybridity' appears in multiple discourses and has layered meanings as well. Midson says "It has its origins in racial theory, but it has also since been taken up in biology, and in technological fields ranging from genetics to engineering.[157] Hybridity as a concept also is prominent in literature, theology, and in critical theory, which includes posthumanism."[158] The understanding of hybridity as a mixing of multiple parts that were typically once separate is important, "For example, hybrid beings that crossover from different species, or hybrid cars that feature both diesel and electric parts."[159] Midson further states, "Etymologically, 'hybridity' comes from the Latin word '*hybrida*'[160] that describes the offspring of a tame sow and a wild boar, which can be deduced as 'mongrel' of sorts and the derogatory connotations of the label 'mongrel' are significant."[161] Midson says,

> For us, the hybrid being appears to be the product of a difference between two parties that is irresolvable other than by recourse to the other 'other', i.e., the third party, the hybrid being itself. Hybridity is, in these cases, predicated on an original emphasis on substantive difference: be it the difference between species, or between types of fuel, or languages, for example.[162]

---

[156] *The Cyborg and the Human: Origins, Creatureliness and Hybridity in Theological Anthropology.*

[157] Scott A. Midson, "The Cyborg and the Human: Origins, Creatureliness and Hybridity in Theological Anthropology" (Ph.D. dissertation, University of Manchester, 2015), 167.

[158] Scott A. Midson, "The Cyborg and the Human," 167.

[159] Scott A. Midson, "The Cyborg and the Human," 167.

[160] "Hybrid," accessed 5 Feb. 2019, www.vocabulary.com/dictionary/hybrid.

[161] Scott A. Midson, "The Cyborg and the Human," 167-168.

[162] Scott A. Midson, "The Cyborg and the Human," 167-168.

Donna Haraway says, "We see something of this in how both fictional and non-fictional stories influence our perceptions of the 'real', the 'real' is a hybrid composed of multiple types of stories that have concrete, material consequences."[163] Bruno Latour, French philosopher, whose work will be pivotal to our study of hybridity, considers technological hybridity,

> As when we find ourselves invaded by frozen embryos, expert systems, digital machines, ...sensor-equipped robots, hybrid corn, data banks, psychotropic drugs, gene synthesisers, audience analysers, cellphones,[164] devices that invade us and so on, when our daily newspapers display all these monsters on page after page, and when none of these chimera[165] can be properly on the object side or on the subject side, or even in between, there arises confusion of categories.[166]

"It is as if there were no longer enough judges and critics to categorize or systematize or make coherent the

---

[163] Donna Haraway, *Modest_Witness@Second_Millennium. FemaleMan_Meets_OncoMouse: Feminism and Technoscience* (London: Routledge, 1997), 2.

[164] Added by the Researcher, not found in the original; quote.

[165] In classical Greek and Egyptian myth, chimeras are depicted as having parts with the morphological characteristics typical of different species. The chimera of Greek mythology, for example, has the head of a lion, the body of a goat, and the tail of a serpent. Not all chimeras are mythical, however. In fact, each one of us is most likely a chimera, according to the modern scientific definition of a chimera as a single organism composed of cells with different embryonic origins (Nagy and Rossant 2001). As we interact with other organisms over the years, their cells become incorporated into our bodies, not through a process of consumption and digestion, but through processes that leave the cells intact. The argument against chimeras most often discussed is the Unnaturalness Argument. It is also the argument against chimeras most often rejected. Taken in its most basic form, the Unnaturalness Argument alleges that because the creation of chimeras is unnatural it is therefore wrong. See "Human/Non-Human Chimeras," in *Stanford Encyclopedia of Philosophy,* accessed 13 Dec. 2018, https://plato.stanford.edu/entries/chimeras/.

[166] Bruno Latour, "Where Are the Missing Masses? The Sociology of Few Mundane Artefacts," in *Shaping Technology/Building Society: Studies in Sociotechnical Change*, edited by Wiebe E. Bijker & John Law (Cambridge, MA.: MIT Press, 1992), 50-51.

hybrids."[167] So, the resistance to neat categorization and systemization is a unique vantage point. The veneration of 'nature' stands contested in the context of proliferating hybrids. With the context of cyberspace, the natural being contested is very important for the sake of engagement. Midson suggests that "Hybridity provides us a significant lens to reconfigure our worldview that is highly dependent on binaries like native/foreigner, nature/culture, real/artificial, etc."[168] The researcher has reviewed the efficacy of hybridity as a methodology and wishes to contest terms like essence, purity, nature, as these concepts place human beings as something special or superior in contrast to creation and world inhabited with technology. Such contestations will facilitate our engagement with technology and cyberspace. As one is used to see thing as substantive or distinctive, hybridity would help in understanding that nothing is obviously distinctive, but co-constitutive. The privilege of original or 'originary' elements stands contested.

3.1.1. Hybridity Contests Substantive and Essentialist Concepts of Purity

Hybridity is read into a substantive context that sees hybridity as the bringing together of otherwise discrete parts. Elaine Graham says, "Consider, for example, Dr. Frankenstein's anxieties about his 'monster' that straddled the boundary between life-and-death."[169] Here, the hybrid being is 'othered' because it disrupts categories of classification. It is 'disorderly' and 'dirty' as structural anthropologist Mary Douglas might see it.[170] Jennifer González discusses, "What makes the term 'hybridity' controversial, of course, is that it appears to assume by definition the existence of a non-hybrid state – a pure state, a pure species, a pure race – with which it is contrasted. It

---

[167] Bruno Latour, *We Have Never Been Modern* (Cambridge: Harvard University Press, 1993), 49-50.

[168] Scott A. Midson, "The Cyborg and the Human," 31.

[169] Elaine L. Graham, *Representations of the Post/Human: Monsters, Aliens and Others in Popular Culture* (New Jersey: Rutgers University Press, 2002), 60.

[170] Mary Douglas, *Purity and Danger: An Analysis of the Concept of Purity and Taboo* (New York: Routledge Classics, 2002), 2.

is the notion of purity that must, in fact, be problematised."[171] Therefore, hybridity as a methodology gives us a lens to transgress substantive and essential categories which acts as stumbling blocks in the Theology-Technology dialogue.

In all the discourse on anthropology, there seems to be there a yearning for an innocent or unadulterated state of humanity. Even the usage of "Humanising Technology" assumes humans as something pristine and technology as something evil. Hybridity debunks the myth that one has substantive, discrete identities, and, stemming from this, we need to refute the notion that hybridity is a "purely contemporary concern."[172] If hybridity is seen as a relatively recent phenomenon, then it will stand vindicated that there was time when humans were not hybrid that we can look back to, an 'Eden' kind of myth to return to. Bruno Latour here therefore contests the understanding of modern. One of the major binaries that such a hybrid way of thinking problematises, is between the remote past and concrete present. For Latour, "When the word 'modern', 'modernisation', or 'modernity' appears, we are defining by contrast, an archaic and stable past."[173] When one talks of technology or cyberspace, philosophy and religion has harked back to an origin of purity, which is seen as glorious. The methodology of hybridity challenges this premise.

3.1.2. Hybridity: Deconstructing the Concept of Nature

Bruno Latour contests 'nature' has never existed as a discrete phenomenon.[174] "Nature and Society have no more existence than West and East. They become convenient and relative reference points

---

[171] Jennifer González, 'Envisioning Cyborg Bodies: Notes from Current Research', in *The Cyborg Handbook*, edited by Chris Hables Gray (London: Routledge, 1995), 275.

[172] Annie Coombes and Avtar Brah, 'Introduction: The Conundrum of 'Mixing," in *Hybridity and its Discontents: Politics, Science, Culture*, edited by Avtar Brah and Annie Coombes (London/New York: Routledge, 2000), 3.

[173] Bruno Latour, *We Have Never Been Modern*, 10.

[174] Bruno Latour, "On Interobjectivity" in *Mind, Culture, and Activity*, Vol. 3, No. 4, (1996), 228-29.

that moderns use to differentiate intermediaries."[175] Latour shows that complex social life predated humans, and therefore humans as social and rest of the creatures as nature is a made up construct which helps in the conversation of cyberspace. Midson opines, "Latour's central argument that we have never been modern – likewise, we have never been natural or even unnatural. Both of these terms presume their counterpoint, whereas no such difference is possible in a vast and broadly-encompassing hybridity."[176] Fukuyama affirms, "Nature broadly seems to suggest a 'givenness.'"[177] This seems obvious in theology as Genesis and the Bible are relatively clear about what is created by God *ex nihilo*. Donna Haraway remarks, "the distinction between nature and culture in the West has been a sacred one; it lies at the heart of the great narratives of salvation history and their genetic transmutation into sagas of secular progress."[178] Midson postulates that "What is needed is a dynamic view of nature that is not entirely indebted to the remote past or to the point of creation."[179] Creation as a worldview and creation used as a literal understanding has to be distinguished as per the researcher. With the help of Peter Scott one arrives at the hybrid situation that does not privilege nature nor demonizes technology. Scott's articulation of the 'postnatural', in short, refers to how "we may neither escape from nature nor are we obliged to conform to it. We are mixed entities participating in a wider environment by way of our machines."[180] Midson beautifully summarises it as follows:

> Scott's understanding of 'nature', via the 'postnatural', explicitly incorporates technology, and as such, the

[175] Bruno Latour, *We Have Never Been Modern*, 85.

[176] Scott A. Midson, "The Cyborg and the Human," 185.

[177] Francis Fukuyama, *Our Posthuman Future: Consequences of the Biotechnology Revolution* (London: Profile Books, 2003), 72.

[178] Donna J. Haraway, "Mice Into Wormholes: A Comment on the Nature of No Nature," in *Cyborgs & Citadels: Anthropological Interventions in Emerging Sciences and Technologies,* edited by G. L. Downey and J. Dumit, (New Mexico: School of American Research Press, 1997), 217.

[179] Scott A. Midson, "The Cyborg and the Human," 186.

[180] Peter Scott, *Anti-Human Theology: Nature, Technology and the Postnatural* (London: SCM Press, 2010), 39.

> dynamism of nature that Peters seeks to affirm is more adequately secured. Moreover, in the degree of flexibility with how we relate in/to the postnatural, there is scope for hybridity, as nothing is static or essentially placed. Instead, there is flux and movement caught within the wider postnatural state, as opposed to a more narrow and rigid understanding of nature.[181]

Therefore, the methodology of hybridity contests all those concepts that is seen as privileged and sacred which is a process in decentering. It helps in understanding technology and cyberspace, not as an accident, corrupt or aberration but as integral to the evolutionary[182] process.

3.2. Cyborg: Hybridity in the Realm of Cyberspace

This section will further explore the hybridity of cyborg theoretically, so as to make the discourse more nuanced and precise.

3.2.1. Articulation of Cyborg

Haraway uses her cyborg figure to call for a new articulation, rather than representation, of the mixity of beings which in her own words, "I have framed the issue in terms of articulation rather than representation. Human beings use names to point to themselves and other actors and easily mistake the names for the things.'"[183] Midson says, "The underlying attitude here is that representation has a tendency towards nominalism, which has traditionally and theologically manifested in *Adamic* and humanocentric terms, where the author of the name exerts a power over the named being."[184] In Genesis, this was expressed as a form of dominanion over animals.[185] Researcher understands that Haraway thinks representation makes

---

[181] Scott A. Midson, "The Cyborg and the Human," 187.

[182] Evolution here does not denote Darwin's Theory of Evolution. Researcher intends organic evolution.

[183] Donna J. Haraway, *The Haraway Reader* (New York: Routledge, 2004), 89.

[184] Scott A. Midson, "The Cyborg and the Human," 187-88.

[185] Gen 2:19.

Cyborg secondary to humanocentricism and therefore articulation could make possible of new stories rather than old stories that venerate the pristine. The cyborg, then, as Haraway articulates it, can be read on one level as a mode of critique of humanocentric thought.[186] For posthumanist theologian Stephen Garner, "the cyborg metaphor stands against perspectives that divide the world into overly simplistic dualisms and hierarchies that are used by those in power to maintain control."[187]

Joseph Schneider says,

> Haraway uses an emphasis on the complex histories of cyborgs to highlight the fusions of different practices, which call into question the universal categories of 'The Machine' and 'The Human.' Previous cyborg figures have inadequately relied on these broad notions in maintaining the unique human at the centre of mechanical and technological augmentations. Thus, we need to recognise that the cyborg, for Haraway, is more nuanced than merely being a metaphor. Instead, 'the cyborg is not only an image or figure, an entity in fact or imagination, but it is also a positioning, a way of thinking and seeing.'[188]

One needs to understand that cyborg as hybrid is an articulation and a positioning that helps in revising some long held binaries and dualisms.

3.2.2. Cultural Cyborg

There are biological and cultural Cyborgs. But, the biological cyborg is beyond the scope of this thesis and therefore cultural cyborg alone will be considered. In the case of the cultural cyborg, the emphasis

---

[186] Donna J. Haraway, *The Haraway Reader* (New York: Routledge, 2004), 89.

[187] Stephen Garner, "The Hopeful Cyborg," in *Transhumanism and Transcendence: Christian Hope in an Age of Technological Enhancement,* edited by Ronald Cole-Turner, (Washington, DC: Georgetown University Press, 2011), 91.

[188] Joseph Schneider, *Donna Haraway: Live Theory* (New York: Continuum, 2005), 61.

is not upon specific examples of technological modification or augmentation of individual human beings, but rather the way in which Western technoculture interacts with the concept of human identity as pointed by Herzfeld.[189] Graham points that through the concept of the cyborg the relationships between human beings, nonhuman nature, cyberspace and machines is explored.[190] Garner says,

> In this cultural sense, Donna Haraway argues, that all people within a technological society and Cyberspace are cyborgs. They may not have technology physically embedded within them, but the boundaries between organism and machine are constantly crossed in everyday social interplay and existence. Technology and Cyberspace shapes every aspect of human life and human identity becomes fluid, being shaped by Techno-Cybercultural forces. One cannot be cut off from their influence.[191]

Haraway says that cyborgs are 'creatures simultaneously animal and machine, who populate worlds ambiguously natural and crafted', and 'we are all chimeras, theorized and fabricated hybrids of machine and organism. In short, we are cyborgs.'[192] The understanding of everyone in the cyberspace as cyborg can be quite destabilizing and helps in understanding the hybrid reality.

3.2.3. Humans as Cyborgs

To explore about humans as Cyborg, Andy Clark says,

> Human beings are 'natural-born cyborgs', that they have a natural inclination to form relationships with technology that expand the human mind outside of the physical

---

[189] Noreen L. Herzfeld, *In Our Image,* 26.

[190] Elaine Graham, *Representations of the Post/Human,* 32.

[191] Donna Haraway, "A Cyborg Manifesto: Science, Technology and Socialist-Feminism in the Late Twentieth Century," in *The Cybercultures Reader,* edited by David Bell and Barbara M. Kennedy (London, New York: Routledge, 2000), 291-292.

[192] Donna Haraway, "A Cyborg Manifesto," 295.

> limitations of the physical body. In effect, the mind 'leaks' out into the technological tools and prostheses that human beings use in everyday life. For we shall be cyborgs not in the merely superficial sense of combining flesh and wires but in the more profound sense of being human technology symbionts: thinking and reasoning systems whose minds and selves are spread across biological brain and nonbiological circuitry.[193]

Garner says,

> Clark argues that it is a mistake to envisage that the most profound and intimate mergers of technology and the human being as involving bodily penetration and, at times, replacement. Prostheses, neural implants, and enhanced perceptual and intellectual systems are the norm for the science fiction cyborg, but the impact of everyday appliances and devices such as cell phones and wristwatches, is a more significant shaper of human identity and behaviour.[194]

Garner points that the vision of cultural cyborg, brings the notion of hybridity sharply into focus where "In the face of NBIC[195] technologies, the boundaries about what is or is not human and non-human begins to blur. If human identity is defined by the relationships that we find ourselves within, then how do the changes that these technologies bring change our notion of what is or isn't part of human nature."[196] Humans as cyborgs challenges the fixity and discrete identity endowed and assumed by human beings.

---

[193] Andy Clark, *Natural-Born Cyborgs: Minds, Technologies, and the Future of Human Intelligence* (New York: Oxford University Press, 2003), 3.

[194] Stephen Garner, "Living in the Borderlands: Cyborgs and the Imago Dei," accessed 13 Dec. 2018, https://www.researchgate.net/publication/242247017_Living_in_the_Borderlands_Cyborgs_and_the_Imago_Dei, 8.

[195] Acronym for the fields of Nanotechnology, Biotechnology, Information technology and Cognitive science.

[196] Stephen Garner, "Living in the Borderlands: Cyborgs and the Imago Dei," accessed 13 Dec. 2018, https://www.researchgate.net/publication/242247017_

3.2.4. Summary

The above explorations has helped in understanding cyborg as a hybrid articulation which gives emphasis and agency to challenge the binaries and dualisms that arise in the context of cyberspace. The understanding of cultural cyborg helps one to view the concept of human being as equally embedded in the technological context and the boundaries of humans, non-humans, machines being rendered as fluid and transgressed in the larger framework of hybridity. The idea of humans as cyborgs highlights that it is not a mutation or aberration, but an inclination of humans to adapt and embody a technological context which makes any talk of privilege or primacy as obsolete.

3.3. Created Co-Creator

The proposal of CCC needs a lot of nuanced understanding. It comes under the functional typology of *Imago Dei*, Stephen Garner helps to set the context for this proposal.

> Joined to the traditional understandings of God's Creation, is the idea that created humanity has a calling from God, seen in the *Imago Dei*, to act creatively within the world as well. In doing this, human beings perform a kind of mediating role in creation, standing between God and the rest of the created order, and this mediation is refined by a love of other human beings and the world. The definitive example of how human beings should live in acting out this agency of creative love is seen in the person, life and death of Jesus Christ, the one who showed how to be fully open to God's call to this vocation.[197]

As Bates points that Stephen Garner's interpretation of Hefner even though maintains the primacy of functional typology, but does retain relational and substantive aspects.[198] The functional interpretation can end up in anthropocentric perspective. Both

---

Living_in_the_Borderlands_Cyborgs_and_the_Imago_Dei, 8.

[197] Stephen Robert Garner, *Transhumanism and the imago Dei,* 188.

[198] Jeanine Thweatt-Bates, *Cyborg Selves,* 144.

Garner and Hefner rely on the concept of relationality of the created co-creator that allows this theological construction to resist techno-optimistic transhumanist quest for biological transcendence and glorification of disembodiment on the one hand and to resist the theological arrogance to refuse the humanity's embeddedness within and kinship with the technonatural world. It is this relationality that helps both of them to see Cyborg as an important theological articulation to engage with, in cyberspace.[199]

The researcher does not see the necessity of retaining the insights of substantive typology as seen in section 2.2.3., but in light of the above discussion sees some merit in the relationality typology as discussed in section 2.2.4. Therefore, CCC even though is basically a functional typology, it sure has certain insights pertinent to relational typology.

3.3.1. Why use Created Co-Creator?

It is the conviction of the researcher that the subject we are dealing is in the domain of Theology-Technology dialogue. As per the reading, many proposals of theories are abstract, either giving technology the primacy or the finitude of human beings as the pivotal axis. Biology is emphasized in some discourses, while creation is given importance in some which makes the dialogue lopsided. But the researcher finds the analysis of Roger A. Willer quite insightful, "Humans are nature. Humans are cultural. Humans are created in the image of God.... The CCC attempts to do justice to the human being as natural and cultural and as created in the image of God. As such, it is, inter alia, a proposal that Hefner offers for public consideration."[200] Philip Hefner puts forward, 'The Created co-creator' as a 'genuine theological construction.' By placing this concept in the wider public arena for consideration and dialogue, Hefner anticipates that it will generate ongoing theological exploration.[201] This balance and

[199] Jeanine Thweatt-Bates, *Cyborg Selves,* 144.

[200] Roger A. Willer, "Created Co-Creator in the Perspective of Church and Ethics," *Zygon: Journal of Religion and Science* Vol. 39 No. 4 (2004), 841-842.

[201] Philip Hefner, "The Evolution of the Created Co-Creator," in *Cosmos as Creation: Theology and Science in Consonance*, edited by Ted Peters (Nashville: Abingdon Press, 1989), 17-19. Hefner notes that communities of faith do not tend

embodied nature of this theory is the reason for its selection. Hefner opines, "Theological affirmations function as possible theories that are accepted, modified or winnowed out entirely according to whether they do in fact help to account for the performance of faith in thought, worship, community life and behavior."[202] His proposal takes the form of following assertions about the place of human beings with respect to God and the world, in the matrix of the interconnections.

3.3.1.1. Understanding of God

Hefner confesses to not having any intention to develop a philosophically sophisticated concept of God.[203] He elaborates, "When I use the term *God,* I refer to that which is ultimate, somewhat in the manner of Paul Tillich, who spoke of God as the "name for that which concerns us ultimately.""[204] He further says "… I most frequently speak, not of ultimate concern, but rather of the *way things really are* and *what really is.* God is the term men and women use to signify that what they are really talking about, what they have come upon in their experience, touches upon the way things really are."[205] Francis Kadaplackal says, "The terms 'the way things really are' and 'what really is' are to be used in reference to God."[206] He was elaborating on the understanding of Philip Hefner. Researcher sees that such an understanding of God is symbolic and therefore dialogically negotiable in the context of cyberspace. But, there are concerns of it being too abstract as well.

---

to think of theology or statements of faith as theories to be tested, instead looking toward insight in the declarative form of revelation. However, he argues that such revelation is typically evaluated in the life and experience of the community, through reflection upon tradition, and the fruit produced by praxis upon that revelation.

[202] Philip Hefner, *The Human Factor,* 19.

[203] Philip Hefner, *The Human Factor*, 32.

[204] Philip Hefner, *The Human Factor*, 32.

[205] Philip Hefner, *The Human Factor*, 33.

[206] Francis Kadaplackal, "In Search of an Adequate Christian Anthropology," in *Technology, Trust, and Religion: Roles of Religions in Controversies on Ecology and the Modification of Life*, Edited by Willem B. Drees (Amsterdam: Leiden University Press, 2009), 131.

3.3.1.2. Paradigm of Jesus

Hefner does not use Jesus strictly in a Christological sense. He tries to make the abstract God-talk into concrete using the example of "Jesus of Nazareth, gleaned chiefly from what is called the Sermon on the Mount."[207] The researcher wishes to paraphrase and summarize what God-talk brings to the experience of the world, the context through Jesus of Nazareth. Hefner says that God as a person or male or parent are quite infantile images but God as personal is emphasized in the 'Sermon of the Mount.'[208] Hefner also says that Jesus portrays the world having a fundamental nature which shows that the world and the context, is not alienated or random, but has coherence.[209] Hefner also emphasizes that Jesus does not consider humans as controlled by God or puppets, but the importance of individual actions is highlighted where individuals count in the larger scheme.[210] This helps in bridging the too literalistic understanding of God revealed as personal through Jesus. It emphasis that the context is not random but has a propensity for coherence and finally the importance of individual action is displayed.

3.3.1.3. Understanding Human Beings

Hefner proposes human beings are understood as natural creatures having come from natural evolutionary processes, and have a constitution endowed by both genetic and cultural material.[211] So, the Evolutionary Biological premise is clear. There is also a natural teleonomy[212] in the human that points to them being biologically

---

[207] Philip Hefner, *The Human Factor*, 84.

[208] Philip Hefner, *The Human Factor*, 85-86.

[209] Philip Hefner, *The Human Factor*, 87.

[210] Philip Hefner, *The Human Factor*, 88.

[211] Philip Hefner, *The Human Factor*, 19.

[212] Collin Pittendrigh proposed the word Teleonomy, to refer to the study of goal directed processes so as to avoid teleological explanations. Teleonomy is the quality of apparent purposefulness and goal-directedness of structures and functions in living organisms brought about by the exercise, augmentation, and, improvement of reasoning. The term derives from two Greek words, τέλος *telos* ("end, purpose") and νόμος *nomos* ("law"), and means "end-directed" (literally "purpose-law"). Teleonomy is sometimes contrasted with teleology, where the latter

formed culture creators, where purpose, meaning and significance is found in this culture-creating context.[213] Hefner also affirms that Created Co-Creator is placed within the "context of the creation and its purposes."[214] This is a unique hybrid situation where humans are placed within the biological evolutionary process, as well as culture-creating context and also placing humans in the theological understanding of creation. Such a position helps in negotiating many theoretical blockades which is a challenge in the milieu of technology and cyberspace.

3.3.1.4. The Present Context

Hefner portrays the context in a very realistic way,

> Planet earth has reached the point where the success of human beings in actualizing who we are – *self-aware creators of culture*-is critical for the entire planetary ecosystem, including the planet's non-human inhabitants. Our present era presents such radical challenges to us that our ability to assess our world and construct frames of meaning that will engender wholesome behavior is seriously destabilized and confused.[215]

Researcher finds that the agency of humans as self-aware creators of culture is emphasized but the radical challenges of the era which destabilizes is the hybrid reference point that triumphs the proposal of Created Co-Creator in a largely destabilizing context like cyberspace.

---

is understood as a purposeful goal-directedness brought about through human or divine intention. Teleonomy is thought to derive from evolutionary history, adaptation for reproductive success, and/or the operation of a program. Teleonomy is related to programmatic or computational aspects of purpose. Cf., "Telenomy," accessed 17 Nov. 2018, https://en.wikipedia.org/wiki/Teleonomy.

[213] Philip Hefner, *The Human Factor,* 20.

[214] Philip Hefner, *The Human Factor,* 39.

[215] Philip Hefner, *The Human Factor,* 20.

3.3.1.5. Myths and Rituals

Hefner historically traces myths and rituals in evolution as "the indispensable bearers of the information that was necessary to suggest, justify and motivate the behavior that would save *Homo sapiens* from destruction."[216] He follows Paul Ricoeur of understanding myth not as a false fable which is the conventional enlightenment thinking. Myth is understood as "(1) a traditional narration which (2) relates to events that happened at the beginning of time and which has the purpose of (3) providing grounds of ritual actions of persons for today and, in a general manner, (4) establishing all the forms of action and thought by which we understand ourselves in our world."[217] Researcher finds this understanding of myth and ritual emphasizing the embodiment of humans in a context where the set of cultural information passed on does not become irrelevant but helps in inhabiting a new context, to thrive and equips in using the religious myth not as an hindrance to emerging contexts but as an engagement and ritual as actions of human formation that give sense of purpose and direction to humans inhabiting it.

3.3.1.6. Relevance to the Context of Cyberspace

Hefner says that "It is science that sets forth the fundamental human teleonomy, but it is myth and ritual that make the basic proposals concerning the direction, meaning, and purpose of the structures and processes whose fulfilment shapes the form of human being."[218] CCC understands anthropology as not just from a scientific teleonomy which can end up to be unchecked technological optimism. Neither does it reduce it to myths and rituals either religious or secular which undermines the technological milieu. The researcher understands the vision of CCC as hybrid that helps in negotiating both worlds and also emphasizing science and religion not as a binary but as integral to being human.

---

[216] Philip Hefner, *The Human Factor,* 20-21.

[217] Philip Hefner, *The Human Factor,* 21.

[218] Philip Hefner, *The Human Factor,* 21.

3.4. Created Co-Creator and Hybridity

The researcher understands the concept of CCC as a hybrid concept. It needs exploring how it will help in the theological anthropological exploration. So, the two concepts have to be taken separately to understand its hybridity.

3.4.1. Humans Being as "Created"

The 'created' in the 'created co-creator' calls for some explanation. Hefner says, "The term 'created' can be understood as our own 'createdness' which affirms that ultimately we are also creatures, and as such, dependent."[219] Vítor Westhelle interpreting the concept of Created Co-Creator, says, "Being created means, therefore, to recognize that we are not that which ultimately brings us about. We are not the cause or origin of our own selves. We can only "see" it, as the apostle Paul says, with the eyes of faith."[220] Francis Kadaplackal says, "Since we are 'created', we belong to 'the way things really are' through our conditionedness and freedom."[221] This also acknowledges the fact that as 'created' beings, we are not the designers of our own place and role in the world. As Hefner says, "to be created is to be derived, to be dependent upon antecedent factors (environmental, biological, cultural) as well as contemporary sources (environmental, cultural)."[222] The term gains its theological significance when we make the reference to 'God,' Hefner suggests the conditionedness of humans where primacy of God and divine creating activity is underlined where God is seen as the ground of creating, out of which humans have emerged.[223] Hefner tries here to integrate the evolutionary and biblical vantage points. Kadaplackal

---

[219] Philip Hefner, "The Evolution of the Created Co-Creator," in *Cosmos as Creation: Theology and Science in Consonance*, edited by Ted Peters (Nashville: Abingdon Press, 1989), 522.

[220] Vítor Westhelle, "The Poet, Practioner and Beholder: Remarks on Hefner's Created Co-Creator," *Zygon, Journal of Religion and Science* Vol. 39, No. 4 (December 2004), 752.

[221] Francis Kadaplackal, "In Search of an Adequate Christian Anthropology," 131.

[222] Philip Hefner, *The Human Factor*, 32.

[223] Philip Hefner, *The Human Factor*, 36.

says that "Created" can be understood as belonging and receptivity and says "the human being has been thought of and understood in dualistic terms."[224] This dualism has been harmful and Hefner says, "we can no longer tolerate understandings of human nature that insist upon separating us from our fellow human beings, from the natural ecosystem in which we live, or from the evolutionary processes in which we have emerged.'[225] Francis Kadaplackal affirms embodiment as integral of our existence. This makes solidarity possible with other human beings which extends the sphere of concern from anthropocentricism to the care of nature and other living beings.[226] The word 'natural' does not imply the sacred natural order, but emphasizes the concept of relationality.

3.4.2. Human Beings Are 'Co-Creators'

Vitor Wishtelle understands 'Co' and Creator in a very unique way. He employs *Poeisis, Praxis* and *Theoria* of Aristotle to the concept of CCC. He understands Created as *Theoria.* Co as Praxis.

> The prefix co-in created co-creator suggests relations, implies mutuality and partnership. Most interpretations of the created co-creator I have seen seem to assume that this partnership is with God alone. I propose that the first inferred meaning of the prefix refers to the human ability to do what we do because we are in human partnership and relations of exchange and interaction within the human community. ... It is an old rabbinic tradition to interpret the first account of the creation of Adam in Genesis as the creation of the first interhuman relationship (*adam* = male + female). And from there it follows that it is this archetypal entity that is endowed with the Image of God, therefore also capable of co-union (communion)

---

[224] Francis Kadaplackal, "In Search of an Adequate Christian Anthropology," 131.

[225] Philip Hefner, "Biocultural Evolution of the Created Co-Creator." *Dialog: A Journal of Theology*, Vol. 36, No. 2 (1997), 198.

[226] Francis Kadaplackal, "In Search of an Adequate Christian Anthropology," 131.

with God. This is what praxis entails: the communicative action and interaction for the sake of doing it well.[227]

The researcher understands the prefix 'co' emphasizing the hybridity which connects person to humans and creation and also with God and therefore critical in theological anthropology. The 'co' in the co-creator has to be emphasized sufficiently if we are to take the term in its right meaning. Peterson says, "This suggests that we are participating in the creative action of God, not on our own, not in subordination, but in partnership. It also confirms that the future is open and undetermined. The human being can give it direction whenever needed, or change the course whenever found necessary. The creative activity of the human being finds its source in God the Creator who gives it to humanity with love. It is characteristic of human beings as 'co-creators' that we can participate actively in the unique plan of God."[228] The researcher observes that the prefix 'co' calls to question stewardship and its primacy in Christian Theology.

The term 'co-creator' may seem to the freedom of the human being, which is a fundamental condition of existence. Richard Fern says, "God grants creation its own, creative freedom for the sake of love, a mutuality that cannot exist apart from genuine freedom and risk. It is not enough to have created creatures with whom he(sic) can talk, creatures capable of grasping creation and analogically, himself in thought, God must give these creatures and, thereby, creation, the nature he has so lovingly made, the capacity to choose their own future, to form and act for reasons, ends, and goals, of their own... Having placed the future of creation in its own reflective awareness, God waits for the free reciprocity of his continuing, sustaining love.[229] Willer suggests that "A careful reading makes clear that human freedom is not the primary value in the thought world of the created co-creator; rather, the elementary value is the furtherance of nature—that is, of the ecological nexus of earth

---

[227] Vítor Westhelle, "The Poet, Practioner and Beholder," 752.

[228] Gregory R. Peterson, "The Created Co-Creator: What it is and is not," *Zygon*: *Journal of Religion and Science,* Vol. 39 No. 4, (2004), 829.

[229] Richard Fern, *Nature, God and Humanity: Envisioning an Ethics of Nature* (Cambridge: Cambridge University Press, 2002), 160.

which is inclusive of the human community but not confined to it. Freedom and transcendence are critical in this."[230] Wishtelle says, "As long as human labor is creative it belongs to the same activity that is also attributed to God, to Jesus, and to the Spirit. This is probably the most scandalous element in Hefner's formulation. It places the human creative activity alongside God's.[231]

Therefore, technology and cyberspace have to be placed in the context of creation and the technological and cyberspace evolution as creative expression, where our role as 'Created Co-Creator' becomes more pronounced. If one takes the evolution of humans into account, we can understand the meaning of nature as follows: '... the appearance of homo sapiens as created co-creator signifies that nature's course is to participate in transcendence and freedom.'[232] The hybridity of CCC helps in engaging with the context and also gives the propensity to transcend it.

3.4.3. Created Co-Creator as a Hybrid Concept that Bridges between Theological and Secular

The researcher wishes to qualify the term 'secular.' Charles Taylor notes "The shift to secularity in this sense consists, among other things, of a move from a society where belief in God is unchallenged and indeed, unproblematic, to one in which it is understood to be one option among others, and frequently not the easiest to embrace."[233] So, secular is seen where the reference to the divine is difficult and cyberspace is such a context. Philip Hefner says,

> That the respective worlds of meaning frequently do not adjust easily to the idea of the created co-creator is the source of the idea's fruitfulness. It is a mistake to overlook this theological/secular possibility, since this possibility accounts for the incendiary and ironic character of the

[230] Roger A. Willer, "Created Co-Creator in the Perspective of Church and Ethics," *Zygon: Journal of Religion and Science*, Vol. 39 No. 4 (2004), 851.

[231] Vítor Westhelle, "The Poet, Practioner and Beholder" 751-52.

[232] Philip Hefner, "Biocultural Evolution of the Created Co-Creator," 197.

[233] Charles Taylor, *A Secular Age* (Massachusetts: The Benkalp Press of Harvard University Press, 2007), 3.

> idea. The idea of the created co-creator is both theological and secular simultaneously; it is not at any moment exclusively one or the other—even though thinkers from either of these perspectives lay their own respective world of meanings upon the idea. The idea cannot be brought fully into play if its double character is ignored, as it almost always is, since theologians are seldom secular-naturalist in their outlook, and conversely secular thinkers are seldom theological in their perspective. The two elements are considered to be alternatives when in fact they ought to understand stereoscopically—two perspectives brought together as one vision.[234]

Peters says,

> The term created co-creator reminds us of a number of important things. First, we are dependent creatures. We depend for our very existence on our cosmic and biological prehistory, and we depend on a still prior desire on God's part to create a world and place us within it. Second, we are creators. We use our cultural freedom and power to alter the course of historical events, and we use our scientific and technological freedom to alter natural events. Third, human beings have a destiny. We have a future toward which we are being drawn by God's will. This makes the concept of the created co-creator an ethical concept—that is, human creative activity is oriented toward our vision of God's will for a renewed creation. Our capacity for creativity is not only a blessing; it is also a moral imperative. We humans created in the Image of God are participants and co-creators in the ongoing work of God's creative activity.[235]

---

[234] Philip Hefner, "Can the Created Co-Creator Be Lutheran?" *Dialog: A Journal of Theology,* Vol. 44, No. 1, (2005), 186.

[235] Ted Peters, "Techno-Secularism, Religion and the Created Co-Creator," *Zygon: Journal of Religion and Science,* Vol. 40, No. 4 (2005), 857.

Creatio Ex Nihilo affirms the ultimacy of God, the creator but not of the 'nature.' The creation also cautions us that one should not have idolatrous expectations from Cyberspace and accompanying technology, but the evolution of cyberspace is permissible as nature is not seen as the Creator. *Creatio Continua* stands as an argument for human intervention seen in the development of cyberspace and the contribution of the intervention of creation where God creates and redeems through future giving, and humans in developing cyberspace are part of the future giving through their creativity.[236] Peters' arguments can be adapted by human development of cyberspace, we have no choice but to creatively express ourselves in the cyberspace and we are not playing God but human, expressed in the creativity espoused in the *imago dei*.[237] Researcher is aware that cyborg anthropology contests a *telos* as seen in section 1.4.1., while CCC talks of a *telos*. This tension is important to understand. One needs to understand the meeting points of these two concepts under hybridity.

3.4.4. Summary

As seen in 3.4.1, the understanding of humans as "Created" has the hybrid understanding from evolutionary biology and biblical creation narrative. This does not privilege humans but see them in continuity with the rest of the creation and cosmos. In 3.4.2, the understanding of Co-Creator is seen not as a privilege but as a gift. The primacy of humans is contested and seen as functional that relates to the whole ecological matrix with the paradigm of being a partner to God in creating and sustaining technology and cyberspace. CCC as a hybrid concept helps in bridging the theological and secular where the biblical understanding of *creatio ex nihilo* is integrated to the scientific endeavor of humans as *creatio continua* which does not place human activity as an aberration but in continuation of the creative mandate.

---

[236] Ted Peters, *Playing God? Genetic Determinism and Human Freedom,* (London: Routledge, 1997), 14-15.

[237] Ted Peters, *Playing God?* 161.

3.5. Hybridity in Cyborg and CCC as a Metaphor of Transgressing Boundaries

Philip Hefner says that crossing boundaries is central to cyborg and CCC. The origin of the idea of Cyborg is a crossing of boundaries.[238] Hefner says,

> Cyborg is to fuse the human and that which is not human, the machine, so as to enable the human to work in an environment that required such a fusion. The boundary between human and technology is transgressed in the very idea. Just so, the Created Co-Creator joins two ideas that are regularly thought to be incomparable-that which is created with that which itself is creator. Such ideas initially cause static in our minds; they are troublesome, not restful.[239]

Hefner points out "Boundary breakdown is signaled in Cyborg's opposition to these commonly held dualisms: nature vs. humans; human vs. animal; nature vs. technology; the organic vs. the machine; the physical vs. the non-physical."[240] Hefner identifies boundary crossing as kinship images of cyborg and CCC, but also pointing,

> However, the encounter with Cyborg reveals most vividly to Created Co-Creator how fully it embodies the fundamental identity of human/nature/culture/technology. This identity pertains to the very terms, "created" and "co-creator." Our createdness, in theological view, is at the hand of God, but at the same time through the emerging processes of nature's and culture's evolution. Createdness stands for kinship with the processes that

---

[238] Philip Hefner, "Created Co-Creator Meets Cyborg," accessed 21 Nov. 2018, https://www.metanexus.net/created-co-creator-meets-cyborg/.

[239] Philip Hefner, "Created Co-Creator Meets Cyborg," accessed 21 Nov. 2018, https://www.metanexus.net/created-co-creator-meets-cyborg/.

[240] Philip Hefner, "Created Co-Creator Meets Cyborg," accessed 21 November 2018, https://www.metanexus.net/created-co-creator-meets-cyborg/.

> have constituted us. To be human is to be this nature. "Co-creator" points to who we are and what we do.[241]

Hefner sharply points, "The electronic technology of computers, the internet, and communications is an expression of our co-creating mind and spirit that is in turn directed toward ourselves, as surely as genetic engineering. Created Co-Creator and Cyborg are sibling images of transgressed boundaries and potent fusions."[242] So, the meeting point of cyborg and CCC through hybridity and its potential has been explored in this section. This unique vantage point equips in transgressing the boundaries of the discourses that either privilege technology as the ultimate *telos* or ones that emphasise the supremacy and centrality of human beings.

3.6. Conclusion

This chapter explored the methodology of hybridity and cyborg as a hybrid concept was further analyzed. CCC helped in grasping the theological anthropology and it gives a direction for action in cyberspace, which the cyborg anthropology alone cannot help. The understanding of CCC as hybrid had to be established for the subject to move forward. The researcher explored how cyborg and CCC were connected through hybridity. As observed, cyborg anthropology helps in interpreting of the context of cyberspace but the direction needed for the search of the authentic Christian human formation can be done by reworking and reformulating the CCC proposal. This chapter presented CCC in the framework of hybridity. But, the next chapter will highlight the limitations of the proposal to rework in the light of Christological engagements.

---

241 Philip Hefner, "Created Co-Creator Meets Cyborg," accessed 21 Nov. 2018, https://www.metanexus.net/created-co-creator-meets-cyborg/.

242 Philip Hefner, "Created Co-Creator Meets Cyborg," accessed 21 Nov 2018, https://www.metanexus.net/created-co-creator-meets-cyborg/.

Chapter 4

Reworking Created Co-Creator in Search of an Authentic Christian Human Formation

Introduction

In the search for an authentic Christian human formation, researcher has used the methodology of hybridity to converse with cyborg anthropology and CCC as seen in chapter three. In Chapter two researcher proposed to employ the Christological lens to theological anthropology, which in this context is the functional typology of *Imago Dei* espoused by CCC. Therefore, the researcher will analyze the drawbacks of the proposed of CCC. The drawbacks will be augmented by engaging with Christological formulations. The Christological engagements will rework the proposal of CCC, which will lead to the authentic Christian human formation in the context of Cyberspace.

4.1. Analyzing the Limitations of the Created Co-Creator Debate

The researcher is aware of the merits of Hefner's CCC proposal, but is also aware of its limitations. The limitations are as follows:

Firstly, the problem that one sees in the proposal is the term 'Co.' which is raised by Gregory R. Peterson.[243] The CCC seems to give an impression that human is showing equality with God which makes the theological anthropology dangerous and uninhibited. As observed in Chapter 3, section 3.4.2., the researcher considers 'Co' as the hybrid space to work upon.

Secondly, the understanding of creation in the proposal is as per evolutionary biology. The evolutionary biology does not have a definite *telos.* Theological anthropology without a definite *telos* is to surrender to the forces of the market. A definite vision of *telos* helps in the aspect of redemption from the context and a Salvation vision to transcend the context. A *telos* is important in the understanding of human formation.

Thirdly, the researcher found there were no particular limits in such a robust theological anthropology which gives emphasis to freedom.[244] In the Context of Cyberspace and technology, such freedom is not unmediated, but is controlled by the market. There needs to be an understanding of limits in any mature theological anthropology if it wishes to foster positive and constitutive human formations.

Fourthly, the understanding of God in CCC is very abstract as the terms *'the way things really are'* and *'what really is'* are to be used in reference to God.[245] Therefore, Incarnation as a premise is important

---

[243] Gregory R. Peterson, "The Created Co-Creator: What It Is and Is Not," *Zygon: Journal of Religion and Science*, Vol. 39, No. 4 (December 2004), 829.

[244] Manuel G. Doncel, "The Kenosis of the Creator and the Created Co-Creator," *Zygon: Journal of Religion and Science*, Vol. 39, No. 4 (December 2004), 791. Doncel does not directly say such a statement, but the researcher deduced it as he offers Kenosis to the understanding of God.

[245] See Francis Kadaplackal , "Created Co-Creator as a Source of Inspiration for a Sustainable Corporate Environmental Responsibility," accessed 20 Jan. 2019, https://www.stthomas.edu/media/cleanupfolder/KadaplackalFinalpa.pdf.

to dialogue to emphasize the embodiment of God revealed in Jesus Christ.

Fifthly, the researcher understands a distinction between optimism and hope. Created Co-Creator espouses optimism which is positive, but not enough. The hope element is very crucial in the search for authentic Christian formation.

Finally, there is a chasm assumed between the Creator and Created. The Created Co-Creator very vaguely tries to bridge it. The earlier noted 'Co' has to be redefined as to know whether the bridging between the Creator and Created is convincing.

Based on the above premise the researcher wishes to first reiterate the context of cyberspace.

4.2. Understanding Cyberspace as a Context for Ministry

This research basically argues that most of the theological discourses tend to make a binary between context (specifically cyberspace in this regard) and church. Conventional understanding of context is seen as fostering inauthentic and dangerous formations that draws one away from God. Church is understood as resisting such inauthentic formations. But, the researcher contests such binaries of context and church. As noted earlier, once the biggest philosophical question was nature, now technology has become the yardstick. This can be said about cyberspace as seen in Chapter three. Cyborg is a hybrid, cultural symbol that signifies human "nature" and is not self-evident. That is, the human body is not completely differentiated from the cyberspace, but the understanding of humans embodied in cyberspace is the articulation of cyborg anthropology where nature is viewed as an emerging process of evolving life that, is now marked by a co-creation among humans and nonhumans, machines and other partners. As seen in Chapter one, one becomes a cyborg when his/her hands touch the mouse or smartphone or earplugs. In viewing human as cyborg, technology is no longer something one uses but it becomes a part of one's self, a prosthesis or an artificial replacement of a body part. Hence, bodies embedded and continuous with gadgets and identities on social media in the cyberspace as Cyborg is the context of ministry which Church will ignore at its own peril. So if cyberspace is the context, there is a need to understand that Christian human formation is closely linked to Christological formulations.

4.3. Christological Reworking of the 'Co'

As seen in 4.1., the researcher wishes to engage the prefix 'Co' as the hybrid space to converse and engage with Christology to reformulate the CCC. On the basis of the above set premise of limitations of the proposal, the researcher would like to converse with various Christological formulations. To begin with the process, cyborg anthropology has been the corollary to Created Co-Creator as seen in Chapter 3. Therefore, the starting line should be to engage with Jeanine-Thweatt-Bates' Cyborg Christ.

4.3.1. Negotiating the Creator-Created Chasm through Divine-Human Debate of Christology

As noted in section 4.1.1., there is a theological chasm between Creator-Created. Christology is the only way one can help understand this chasm and bridge it. The divine-human debate is a Christological problem which makes debates or anthropological implications next to non-dialogical as these two realms are seen as separate compartments that is unique and separate substance that is non-negotiable. The researcher would take the aid of Jeanine Thweatt-Bates proposal of Cyborg Christ to reconfigure the debate. Bates starts with an interesting premise, "Destabilizing what it means to be human as seen in Cyborg troubles what it means for God to become human. This might seem overtly threatening but Kull sees it as Theological and Christological Opportunity."[246] Bates continues to raise some critical concerns in the light of traditional Christology:

> The hybridity of the cyborg Christ, in light of the traditional Christological definition of Chalcedon,[247]

[246] Jeanine Thweatt-Bates, *Cyborg Selves: A Theological Anthropology of the Posthuman,* (New York: Routlledge, Taylor and Francis, 2012), 175.

[247] The Council of Chalcedon in 451 A.D. expressed this largely universal view by asserting that Jesus Christ was one 'hypostasis' (ὑποστάφσις) who had two natures (φύσεις), a divine nature and a human nature, joined together, so that 'at no point was the difference between the natures taken away though the union,

> prompts a reconsideration of the substantive notions of both humanity and divinity. Reconstruction of not just the ontological category of the "human," but also concepts of personal identity from a posthuman perspective also opens up new possibilities for answering persistent age-old Christological questions regarding the question of the unity of Christ's person and divine/human status. Here we see that Christology redefines the concept of humanity as the question of Christ's ultimate humanity, as a divine figure who is simply not human, but opens a greater space to interrogate it.[248]

But, still there is a question that needs answering is what is the foundation of divine-human debate that made it such a complicated non-dialogical impasse? F. LeRon Shults says that the over dependence of the philosophical category of substance based on Aristotelian categories is the reason for assumed purity concepts which was opposed to any form of hybridity.[249] The researcher considers that the understanding of substance is irrelevant to the present understanding where the Aristotelian philosophical method does not hold. Stephen Garner asserts that "God became enfleshed in the person of Jesus of Nazareth, the incarnation is a paradox of hybrid existence. In Jesus Christ both human and divine natures were united in hypostatic union that brought together two different realities and held them in tension as a unified identity."[250] Garner retains the word hypostatic, but uses it in the sense of the divine

---

but rather the property of both natures is preserved and comes together into a single person and a single subsistent being. 'Christ had 'a rational soul and a body', and - Chalcedon seems to be saying- his humanity consisted in his having these. See Richard Swirnbine, "The Coherence of The Chalcedonian Definition of the Incarnation," accessed 7 Mar. 2019. http://users.ox.ac.uk/~orie0087/pdf_files/Papers%20from%20Philosophical%20Journals/Swinburne_2011-incarnation.pdf, 1.

[248] Jeanine Thweatt-Bates, *Cyborg Selves,* 175.

[249] F. LeRon Shults, *Christology and Science* (Grand Rapids, MI, 2008), 23.

[250] Stephen Garner, "Transhumanism and the Imago Dei: Narratives of Apprehension and Hope" (Ph.D. Dissertation, The University of Auckland, 2006), 239-240.

and human realms interpenetrating each other. The researcher feels Arthur Peacocke proposal of incarnations as, 'Transcendence-in-immanence', would help in giving more clarity and direction. which Peacocke says,

> Incarnation may be understood as the fulfilment of transcendence-in-immanence of human religious experience that raises the hope and conjecture that in man, in a human person adequate for the purpose, immanence might be able to display in a uniquely emergent mode a transcendent dimension to a degree which could unveil, without distortion, the transcendent Creator.[251]

The above understanding of Incarnation shows the penetration of transcendence-in-immanence where immanence or context is seen as worthy of revealing the transcendent Creator and thereby effectively negotiating the Creator-Created chasm. With the help of Cyborg Christ and "Transcendence-in-Immanence" proposal, both a methodology of hybridity, helped cross the impasse of Creator-Creator, not in the ontological sense but in the sense of ethics and praxis.

4.3.2. Emphasizing Materiality and Creatureliness through Christological Formulations

Cyberspace being a material reality has the danger of being simplistically spiritualized as a context that is evil in popular discourses in the Church. Researcher does not wish to absolutize the Cyberspace. But in the search for human formation, one needs to know if the context is redeemable? The debate of Christology espoused by Anne Kull can give direction in this regard. Kull's embrace of Jesus as "hybrid creature is an attempt to articulate resistance to an otherworldly divine perfection"[252] What is meant here is the negative binary of the material context in contrast to the divine. Bates underscores that

[251] Arthur R. Peacocke, *God and the New Biology* (London: Dent, 1986), 132.

[252] Anne Kull, "Cyborg Embodiment and Incarnation," 284.

> Kull's interpretation underscores the way in which boundaries between spiritual and material, divine and human, are being redrawn in the figure of Christ. As a divine/human hybrid, The Cyborg Christ defines each and every term. The Cyborg Christ, as Kull's description of Jesus as "hybrid creature" indicates an affirmation of hybridity also means a redemption of creatureliness, a healing of unnecessary rift between materiality and spirituality. So, creatureliness is not seen as corrupting the divine and creatures are not doomed to be seen as opposites of divine.[253]

This helps in further reiterating that the substance category of divine and human nature is seen irrelevant in Christological deliberations where creatureliness and materiality is seen as important in the dialogue that makes the Cyborg Christ proposal fluid.

Taking into cognizance the dichotomy of 'Jesus of history and Christ of faith'[254] Kwok Pui-Lan helps in negotiating it. Bates quotes, "Kwok Pui-Lan points to the borderland between the human and divine, as she uses the slash in writing "Jesus/Christ" to indicate that the human/divine boundary is unfixed and fluid, contested and constructed, which is positive and necessary."[255] Kwok says that

> The notion of Jesus/Christ has been a hybrid concept from the very beginning, and there is no original, privileged understanding of Christ that can be claimed as pure and foundational and that explosion of hybrid images of Jesus are the expressions of the struggle for the articulation of identity of formerly colonized and oppressed peoples,

---

[253] Jeanine Thweatt-Bates, *Cyborg Selves,* 181.

[254] The question includes issues regarding the relationship of an academic study of Jesus and a confessional affirmation of Jesus. It is also part of the larger question regarding how to understand the humanity of Jesus and the divinity of Jesus in speaking about Jesus as the God-man. See Martin Kahler, *So-called Historical Jesus and the Historic, Biblical Christ,* translated by Carl E. Braaten (Philadelphia: Fortress Press, 1964).

[255] Jeanine Thweatt-Bates, *Cyborg Selves,* 181.

> and further, that as the identity of a group becomes more fluid and diversified, a more nuanced and diverse Christology emerges.[256]

The above observation has helped in making the inferior view of materiality and creatureliness, as a faulty premise. There are also theological understanding of human *Imago Dei* being corrupted due to original sin[257] and original sin deems creatureliness and materiality as inferior. According to such a premise, the work of Christ is seen as returning humans to the original state of innocence. Such faulty premise create naïve response to human responsibility and view formation in a negative sense. Again the challenges of hybridity seen in Chapter 3 in section 3.2, is used as lens to contest the understanding of original, pure, perfect et al. This revision helps to understand human formation that affirms creatureliness and materiality because of the Christological formulations expressed above. Hence, returning to a so called original state or spiritualizing the material reality is not the option. Therefore, if moving back to the original is not the option, what is the other alternative?

4.3.3. Reworking the *Telos* through Omega Point and Christology

Taking the cue from the question left unanswered in the above section, the answer of the movement if not backward to something original, is to move towards a *Telos.* As pointed in 4.1., CCC is based on evolutionary biology. But, the evolutionary biology and its vision of randomness alone cannot help in the direction of the research.

---

[256] Pui-Lan Kwok, *Postcolonial Imagination,* 182-183.

[257] Five elements of the doctrine of original sin are as follows: (1) the source of original sin is a primal sin in the garden of Eden. (2) All human beings share in this sin because of our solidarity with Adam, the progenitor of the race. The results of the primal sin are twofold. (3) From birth, all human beings have an inherited sin (original sin itself), which comes in two forms: common guilt, and a constitutional fault of disordered desire and ignorance. (4) In addition, Augustine holds that the human race suffers a penalty because of sin—human powers are weakened, and we will experience death. (5) Finally, Augustine speculates about how both sin and penalty are transmitted from generation to generation. See Jesse Couenhoven, "St. Augustine's Doctrine of Original Sin," *Augustinian Studies* 36:2 (2005), 363

Therefore, Pierre Teilhard de Chardin is important to the discussion as he is an important voice in Evolutionary Biology. Denis Edwards says that Teilhard's "personal discovery of evolution enabled him to begin to see how matter is the matrix of the spirit and spirit is the higher state of matter."[258] In some worldviews matter is emphasized while others make spirit the ultimate, however hybridity of matter and spirit brings them both in an engagement. "What became central for him was the conviction that the evolutionary law of complexity consciousness does not stop with biosphere but continues into noosphere, the sphere of human mind and of interpersonal consciousness and love."[259] Vincent Marasigan says that the concept of Noosphere and the development of Cyberspace is related.[260] Edwards opines that Teilhard "became convinced that the evolution now takes the form of a movement toward a global convergence and union of the human, to a point of irreversibility that he called Omega. He saw the universe, the whole world of matter, as in the process of becoming fully personalized in this Omega point."[261] Teilhards says that the Omega point is the "Prime mover ahead, an energizing force of love that attracts all things towards itself. But the Omega is not just in the future, it is really present. To be supremely active, Omega must be supremely present."[262] This is the *Telos* that the researcher

[258] Denis Edwards, "Teilhard's Vision As Agenda for Rahner's Christology," in *From Teilhard to Omega:Co-Creating an Unfinished Universe,* edited by Ilia Delio (Bangalore: Theological Publication of India, 2014), 53.

[259] Denis Edwards, "Teilhard's Vision as Agenda for Rahner's Christology," 53.

[260] Vincent Marasigan, "Teilhard Recalled," *Landas* Vol. 11 (1997): 199. The noosphere is a planetary thinking network — an interlinked system of consciousness and information, a global net of self-awareness, instantaneous feedback, and planetary communication. At the time of his writing, computers of any merit were the size of a city block, and the Internet was, if anything, an element of speculative science fiction. Yet this evolution is indeed coming to pass, and with a rapidity, that in Gaia time, is but a mere passage of seconds. In these precious moments, the planet is developing her cerebral cortex, and emerging into self-conscious awakening. We are indeed approaching the Omega point that Teilhard de Chardin was so excited about.

[261] Denis Edwards, "Teilhard's Vision as Agenda for Rahner's Christology," 53.

[262] Pierre Teilhard de Chardin, *The Phenomenon of Man* (New York: Harper and Row, 1976), 269.

said in the first section. As Cyborg method employed in the research is Non-Teleological, so as to circumvent the theological trap of Original Sin and the myth of a pure and innocent state like Eden to return to. But a good vision of a *Telos* like the Omega point is imperative in this research.

One wonders what is the Christological element in this proposal. Edwards says "Teilhard has a concept of Christic which says of a God as not simply as God above, but as God ahead, the God who draws all things to their completion in Christ. The incarnation of God in Christ in Jesus Christ reveals an Image of God who is radically involved in matter. The risen Christ sharing in the divine immensity, is at work in the whole creation."[263]

Edward continues,

> There is more in the total Christ than humanity and divinity. There is also whole creation. Teilhard speaks of creation as a third aspect of the function of Christ, as in a true sense of the word, a third nature of Christ... The union between the Omega of evolution and Christ constitutes a divine milieu in which all opposition between universal and personal is wiped out... For Teilhard, then, cosmogenesis reveals itself first in biogenesis and then in noogenesis, and culminates only in true christogenesis.[264]

Christogenesis through the Christic is the full revelation of the incarnated Christ as Image of God revealed in matter and space. The engagement of evolution with Omega point and the culmination of the process as Christogenesis where true humanity is found is a hybrid proposal. To have a purposeful formation of human as Christological works out the *Imago Dei* where God is involved and embodied, which counters the abstract "That which is" God understanding used by Hefner. The understanding of

---

[263] Denis Edwards, "Teilhard's Vision as Agenda for Rahner's Christology," 53-54.

[264] Denis Edwards, "Teilhard's Vision as Agenda for Rahner's Christology", 54-55.

creation moving to a purposeful end in Omega Point is similar to the Orthodox concept of 'Theosis'[265] which avoids the problem of original sin. So, the Salvation understanding through this Christology helps in a positive and purposeful formation where the salvation in the context of cyberspace is the movement towards the Christic possibilities culminating in Christogenesis or to conform to the *Imago Dei* seen in the Omega Point.

4.3.4. Introducing Limits through Kenotic Christology

As observed earlier, unbridled freedom in the proposal of CCC seems to be a dangerous outcome. This needs to be addressed. The researcher finds Kenosis Christology appropriate in this attempt. Now the question is how is Kenosis Christology part of the *Imago Dei?* Roman Guridi answers "reading the imago Dei through the lens of the notion of kenosis is not only reasonable, but it is also a theological requirement if one wants to be faithful to the biblical data and to the intimate connection between Christology and anthropology."[266] He further adds "the New Testament is not only emphatic in pointing to Christ as the true Image of God (2 Cor 4:4 and Col 1:15), but it also emphasizes that whoever has seen Jesus, has seen the Father (John 14:9), and that Jesus is the one who reveals the Father (Mt 11:27)."[267] In this sense Kenosis is connected to *Imago*

---

[265] Theosis is the belief, mostly found within the Eastern Orthodox Church, that Christians can experience a union with God and become like him so much that they participate in the divine nature. This concept is also known as deification. Theosis does not mean that they become Gods or merge with God but that they are deified. They participate in the "energies" of God with which he reveals himself to us in creation. But, these Christians are said to not participate in God's essence. Furthermore, this deification does not mean that a person stops sinning or no longer struggles with sin. Instead, theosis is a mystical union with God that proceeds throughout the person's life and culminates in the resurrection of the body. Some have said that this is equivalent to sanctification as taught in the Western churches. See Matt Slick, "What is Theosis" *CARM,* accessed 7 Mar. 2019, https://carm.org/what-is-theosis.

[266] Roman Guridi, "Imago Dei as Kenosis: Re-imagining Humanity in an Ecological Era" (Ph.D. dissertation, Boston College, School of Theology and Ministry, 2016), 148.

[267] Roman Guridi, "Imago Dei as Kenosis," 149.

Dei and will help in revising the proposal of CCC. Manuel G. Dolce says, "The Christian idea of kenosis ("self-emptying") is conceptually and etymologically grounded in the New Testament hymn verse in Philippians 2:7: 'Rather he (Jesus the Christ) emptied himself (*heauton ekenosen*), taking the form of a slave, coming in human likeness" (NAB). This kenosis has been traditionally applied to the incarnated Logos."[268] The original proposal here tries to associate the Kenosis to the Creator. The researcher differs in this approach and rather takes the Logos Understanding of John 1 "Through him all things were made, without nothing was made that has been made."[269] Jesus through Logos reveals a new understanding of the process of Creation and Creator, where the act of Creation is not seen as power, but an act of love.[270] Docel says, "Thus, we can imagine the kenosis of the Creator as a self-restriction of divine being, freely realized in loving respect for the creatures that are to be created. Such self-restriction is required in order to offer to creatures metaphysical play, so that they can exist and act as autonomous created beings."[271] The researcher modifies Docel's statement as follows: "The most momentous element of this Kenosis Christology attached to Creation through Logos, is related to our human actions, or actions of any free responsible beings, wherever they reside."[272] Dennis Edwards writes, "Real freedom is the freedom to enter into love, to risk oneself with another. . . . And the Kenotic Christ revealed in trinitarian God is ...

---

[268] Manuel G. Doncel, "The Kenosis of the Creator and the Created Co-Creator," *Zygon*: *Journal of Religion and Science,* Vol. 39, No. 4 (December 2004), 792.

[269] John 1:3.

[270] Manuel G. Doncel, "The Kenosis of the Creator and the Created Co-Creator," 792, The quote is modified to keep the consistency of emphasis on Christology.

[271] Manuel G. Doncel, "The Kenosis of the Creator and the Created Co-Creator," 793.

[272] Manuel G. Doncel, "The Kenosis of the Creator and the Created Co-Creator," 793.

free beyond comprehension to enter into the vulnerability of loving communion"[273]

The question is, what does this understanding brings to the fore? The responsibility to imitate Christ is imperative Doncel states,

> Because we are created in God's image, we should imitate God. Our kenosis is an expression of the love principle and should also mark all human and technological activity as co-creators. We have in the past understood wrongly the biblical text about our dominion over the world (Genesis 1:28), and that misunderstanding is the result of our faulty idea of God and God's dominion. We should learn from God's lovingly self-restricting respect for all creatures and so follow the command to "cultivate and care for the Garden of Eden (Genesis 2:15 NAB).[274]

So, Kenotic Christology revealing the Image of God through Christ, helps in redefining 'freedom' and imitating Jesus who through his incarnation revealed that entering limitation or a situation of vulnerability is an act of love. So, the understanding of the act of Creation as power has to be redefined as an act of love, and therefore a call to create with love and care, specifically in the context of cyberspace. The God revealed in such an Incarnation is not an abstract God, but an embodied God who is not just shown as almighty, but also as vulnerable, and this paradox is important in the human formation.

4.3.5. Introducing Hope through Christological Dimensions of Resurrection and Eschatology

As explained in the initial premise, there is a difference between optimism and hope. Optimism is connected to the context which

---

[273] Denis Edwards, "Discovery of Chaos and the Retrieval of Trinity" in *Chaos and Complexity Scientific Perspectives on Divine Action,* edited by Robert John Russel, Nancey Murphy and Arthur R. Peacocke, (Vatican City State: Vatican Observatory Publications, and Berkeley: Center for Theology and Natural Sciences, 1995), 446.

[274] Manuel G. Doncel, "The Kenosis of the Creator and the Created Co-Creator," 797.

helps in navigating it effectively. But, that is not sufficient. Hope helps one to transcend the context which is also one of the concerns in human formation. Ted Peters employs Robert John Russel who adds resurrection and schatology to CCC. Researcher feels redemption is important to *Imago Dei* and resurrection and eschatology is the Christology that reveals the true *Imago Dei* through Christ. This is very critical for the same or else one resigns to the forces that shape Cyberspace, namely the market. Ted Peter's says,

> Russell turns our attention to the radical newness of what we have witnessed in the resurrection of Jesus. Yesterday's Easter resurrection and tomorrow's new creation are transformations that require an action by God, something we cannot imagine as a natural evolutionary development or as the product of human creativity alone. Human creativity is not alone, however; it is accompanied by God's ongoing creativity.[275]

Russel connects resurrection to the eschatology where he notes, "It is this eschatological future—no matter how dim, how inconceivable it is in light of science, no matter how unlikely it is in light of evil and suffering in human society and in nature—to which we must orient all our ultimate plans and ideals and convictions if we are to live as Christians today in the Easter dawning of a new age."[276] Eschatology is also seen as the revealing of *Imago Dei* in Christ as Jason Roberts notes, "The eschatological interpretation of the Image of God, based on the New Testament portrayal of Jesus Christ as the quintessential image or icon of divinity, can be read as an extension of the functional-royal interpretation, since "image" passages in the New Testament characterize Christ as the redeeming "Lord" who reveals and inaugurates God's righteous reign on earth as in heaven."[277] This fits well with CCC, as it too is Functional

---

[275] Ted Peters, "Techno-Secularism, Religion and the Created Co-Creator," *Zygon: Journal of Religion and Science* Vol. 40, No. 4, (2005), 858-859.

[276] Robert John Russell, "Five Attitudes toward Nature and Technology from a Christian Perspective," *Theology and Science* 1, No. 2 (October 2003), 157.

[277] Jason Roberts Paul, "Emerging in the Image of God: From Evolution to Ethics in a Second Naïveté Understanding of Christian Anthropology," (Ph.D.

Typology of *Imago Dei.* Moltmann reiterates, "Jesus resurrection is the appearance of this eternal life and his coming draws all this into his future, so that they may become new and participate in the feast of God's eternal joy."[278] Russel's crucial interpretation can be paraphrased as the eschatological perspective no matter how distant in future or slow in invading the ordinary world "…technology must ultimately serve as a means to express and help achieve this future, even if in a very rudimentary way."[279]

This redirects the ethics of technology and the users of technology in the given milieu of Cyberspace. Also, one is aware resurrection and eschatology, in popular theology seems to advocate an evacuation plan from the world and its contexts. N. T. Wright says,

> For the early Christians, the resurrection of Jesus launched God's new creation upon the world, beginning to fulfill the prayer Jesus taught his followers, that God's kingdom would come "on earth as in heaven" (Matt. 6:10), and anticipating the "new heavens and a new earth" (Isa. 65:17, 66:22; 2 Pet. 3:13; Rev. 21:1) promised by Isaiah and again in the New Testament. …heaven is undoubtedly important, but it's not the end of the world. The early Christians were not very interested, in the way our world has been interested, in what happens to people immediately after they die.[280]

This understanding of the world as New Creation calls for taking the context very seriously. Researcher understands the present as a hybrid space between resurrection where the New Creation was released and Eschatology or *Paraousia* that is the hopeful future that

---

dissertation, Marquette University, 2009), 162.

[278] Jurgen Moltmann, *The Coming of God,* translated by Margaret Kohl (Minneapolis: Fortress Press, 1996), 336.

[279] Robert John Russell,. 2003. "Five Attitudes toward Nature and Technology from a Christian Perspective," 157.

[280] N. T. Wright, "Jesus Is Coming: Plant a Tree," accessed 29 Jan. 2019, https://www.plough.com/en/topics/justice/environment/jesus-is-coming-plant-a-tree.

invades our present and informs it. The reworking of hope is the premise one gets here and in a Cyberspace saturated with one gadget replacing the other, or new things being the obsession, Resurrection and Eschatology help us to understand that a consumer understanding of newness will lead humans to doom. But the understanding of newness is associated with new creation that calls us to have ethics of beneficence[281] that is life giving, revitalizing and invigorating.

4.4. 'Co' as the Christological Hybridity that Reformulates Created Co-Creator

It is the conviction of the researcher that by Christological reworking the 'Co' as the hybrid space, the following proposals will help in arriving at an authentic Christian human formation.

4.4.1. Searching the Divine as the Possibility of Ultimate Humanity

Chasm between Creator and Created is understood as ontological which made any dialogue impossible. Using the Divine-Human debate of Christology, as seen in section 4.3.1., Cyborg Christ transcending the divine human binary, as a hybrid figure that reveals ultimate potential of humanity. When one reworks 'Co' in the light of Cyborg Christ, it is seen as a Jesus Christ as revealing the possibility of Ultimate humanity, not as something to reach a mark, but an image to grow into. It is the hybrid space where humanity of Christ informs God and Divinity of Christ informs humans, where the possibility of growth is seen. This sets the premise and context for the formation. Arthur Peacocke's 'Transcendence-in-immanence' understanding of incarnation reworks Incarnation as a doctrine. So, the + in this understanding is not seen as once and for all, historic event, but the original Incarnation is a call for the "Transcendence-in-immanence" possibility of humans in the given context which the

---

[281] Beneficence is defined as an act of charity, mercy, and kindness with a strong connotation of doing good to others including moral obligation. See Frank Stuart Kinsinger, "Beneficence and the Professional's Moral Imperative." *Elsevier* (1st April 2010) accessed 7 Mar. 2019, https://www.ncbi.nlm.nih.gov/pmc/articles/PMC3342811/.

researcher feels is the real meaning of "On earth as it is in Heaven" in the Lord's prayer, especially in the context of Cyberspace. The fear of 'Playing God' has been pronounced in the realm of technology and Cyberspace. But the reworking of 'Co' helps in understanding that it is part of being human to grow and evolve in a given context searching for the divine possibilities, without assuming to be God. This fosters a human formation which does not have a sacred/ profane dichotomy, but searches with responsibility the possibilities to be the Image of God in Cyberspace.

4.4.2. Redemption of Materiality and Creatureliness Espouses New Ethics

Cyborg Christ portrays an Incarnation that shows an *Imago Dei* where the creatureliness or Created is redeemable and the distinction between material and spiritual is seen as superfluous as observed in section 4.3.2. This reworking makes the 'Co' to espouse a theological anthropology that has a material understanding of humanity that can be redeemed. It does not make a transcendence-immanence dichotomy as a top down approach. So the context of Cyberspace is not negated by talking of escape, neither is it seen as the ultimate, but understood as redeemable comprehending human vocation as disciples of Jesus. The 'Co' worked out helps in negotiating the space between humans, and machines, between humans and cyberspace that calls for engaging with the materiality of the cyberspace. This logically helps in collapsing the distinction between able bodied and disabled bodied. The disabled bodies aided by prosthetics, gives a new hermeneutics where nobody is seen as perfect or normal, but all are dialogical and engaging. A much more compassionate formation emphasizing the agency of the people is observed. This calls for an inclusive community formation as well.

4.4.3. Encountering the Limits through Kenotic Christology

The danger of 'Frankenstein' monster'[282] informs the discourse on technology. Reworking the 'Co' with the help of Kenotic

[282] A character in the novel Frankenstein, or the Modern Prometheus (1818) by Mary Shelley. Frankenstein is a scientist who creates and brings to life a manlike

Christology highlights the understanding that Christ is the *Imago Dei* revealed in Kenosis Christology who chose the downward movement, without claiming equality as seen in section 4.3.3. It shows the possibility of limitations, vulnerability and the power of love to be employed as a check in cyberspace. 'Co' helps for a human formation that understands the reality of limitation and suffering over the vision of unbridled freedom. It calls for a formation where humans are called to a downward movement that helps in seeing the context of cyberspace as one to engage in vulnerable situations to uplift the people, to work in love and to bring a connection that fulfills the mandate of 'Loving God and Loving neighbours.'[283] The reworking shows *Imago Dei* is not in the images of glory, power and the spectacular works which is the temptation the contexts compels humans to perform. It shows that true Image of God is revealed in Christ who entered into limitations, taking the lived reality very seriously through public ministry of healing and empowering. A different trajectory of human formation becomes possible where the potentials and dangers of freedom are comprehended and a choice to act responsibly and imitating Christ is highlighted.

4.4.4. Understanding the *Telos* through Omega Point and Christogenesis

As discussed above in 4.3.4., the evolutionary biology which is the foundation of CCC emphasizes randomness. This can lead to unhealthy human formations along with a sense of indifference. The Omega point shows a purposeful *telos* without depending on Original

---

monster which eventually turns on him and destroys him; Frankenstein is not the name of the monster itself, as is often assumed. See "Frankenstein," in *English Oxford Living Dictionaries,* accessed 28 Feb. 2019, https://en.oxforddictionaries.com/definition/frankenstein. Researcher uses the term to express the anxiety that the technology humans create will one day destroy them.

[283] Jesus replied: "'Love the Lord your God with all your heart and with all your soul and with all your mind. This is the first and greatest commandment. And the second is like it: 'Love your neighbor as yourself.' All the Law and the Prophets hang on these two commandments." (Matt 22: 37-40. N.I.V.) Quoting the Bible verse the researcher has compressed it to the basic elements of Loving God and Loving neighbor).

sin or a tendency to return to innocent 'Eden.' Christogenesis is the *Imago Dei* revealed in Christ at the omega point leads every creative act as salvific and the context taken as a divine milieu. In a market mediated cyberspace, to have undefined ends or goals is dangerous where Christogenesis calls for a human formation that aligns with the hopeful vision of all flourishing of the creation, not just humans. The term Christogenesis can be understood as turning every activity one does to grow into the Image of God revealed in Christ as the Omega Point. Therefore cyberspace becomes a context where the engaging activity of humans has to consider the ecology and the well beings of all creatures as understood as Christic seen above. It is a call for *Tikum Olam*[284] where interbeing[285] with the whole creation is fostered. It also reveals a God who is not abstract as noted above in the proposal of CCC, but is imaged as a lover who longingly calls us forward to an embodied reality.

4.4.5. The Dimension of Hope through Resurrection and Eschatology

The category of optimism is popular in discourse of technology which also seemed to be the case of CCC. The dimension of hope added to 'Co' as a hybrid space between resurrection and eschatology is significant. Resurrection and eschatology conventionally understood, inspires a disengagement with material realities of the world as humans should care for a glorious life after death. But, as observed in 4.3.5., the resurrection of Jesus is not just a reality that affects humans after death alone, but is a radical reality of the present which is important to human formation. This understanding helps

---

[284] Hebrew Understanding of repairing the broken world, bringing it closer to the harmonious state for which it was created. See Tzvi Freeman, "What Is Tikkun Olam," *Chabad.Org*, accessed 28 Feb. 2019, https://www.chabad.org/library/article_cdo/aid/3700275/jewish/What-Is-Tikkun-Olam.htm.

[285] A state of connectedness and interdependence of all phenomena. Thich Nhat Hanh a Buddhist Monk who coined the word says "To be" is always to "inter-be." If we combine the prefix "inter" with the verb "to be," we have a new verb, "inter-be." To inter-be reflects reality more accurately. We inter-are with one another and with all life." See Thich Nhat Hanh, *The Art of Living* (London: Rider, 2017), 13.

in having a new urgency in the 'present.' As part of the New Creation, there is a great responsibility to do things with ethics of beneficence as the eschatology that one awaits is invading the present, so every act or technology or engagement in cyberspace is seen as working towards that eschatological and hopeful reality. It is a hopeful possibility that gives human formation a sense of urgency. It is seen as revelation of the *Imago Dei* that is partially revealed through human actions in the given context. It does not rely on optimism that has market value overtones which is dangerous as seen in transhuman vision, but highlights hope which is a directive force to a purposeful human formation.

4.5. Conclusion

The researcher attempted in pointing out the limitations of the CCC proposal. Christological engagement with the Created Co-Creator was used to redress the lacunae in the original proposal. The strands of Cyborg Christ, Omega Point and Christology, Kenotic Christology and Resurrection and Eschatology helped in building a theological anthropology that is consistent with the context of Cyberspace. It carves out a hybrid space for the Authentic Christian Human formation which will be useful in understanding Mission, Ministry and *Ecclessia.* This will be explored in the final conclusion.

Final Conclusion

The study attempted to arrive at the authentic Christian Human formation by reworking Created Co-Creator through Christological Hybridity. The researcher would like to conclude as how these human formations help in understanding Ecclesia, Ministry and Mission.

Human Formation and *Ecclesia*

The understanding of *Ecclesia* that is neatly contained in the 4 walls of the Church is contested. *Ecclesia* is understood as a community that searches for possibilities of finding the divine in the mundane where the sacred/profane dichotomy is nullified. The conventional *ecclesia* is captive of morality and boundaries which the reworked human formations challenge. *Ecclesia* is a space that does not privilege normal human bodies but includes disabled bodies and people with intellectual disabilities. This also includes challenging the normativity of patriarchy and heteronormativity. With the encounter of limits, the *Ecclesia* is seen as a compassionate community that expresses solidarity rather than establish boundaries to exercise power. Such an understanding of *Ecclesia* does not make an ethnic exclusive superior claims of believers. It is a a community that celebrates the diversity espoused in the Kingdom of God, including everyone with a *Telos* to move towards which the Cyberspace has made possible to imagine and to embody it in reality.

Human Formation and Ministry

Ministry involves activities conventionally understood as associated with the *Ecclesia.* Based on the reworked human formations in the context of cyberspace, engaging with the ethos of Cyberspace is seen as imperative. The potential of cyberspace is not seen as a threat or a binary to *Ecclesia*, neither is it surrendered to the forces of the market in the form of unbridled freedom. The numerical growth of Churches or church planting is not seen as ministry. The scope of ministry is seen everywhere in a Post-Secular ethos. Therefore, catering to the doctrinal Christian believers alone cannot be ministry. Researcher believes that 'Public theology'[286] becomes prominent where ministry is not a top down patronizing control mechanism, but a space for engagement and dialogue with believers, people beyond the boundaries of faith and people who do not have any interest in faith. The ministry is to be incarnated, to have the downward movement of building the community in solidarity in midst of vulnerability and brokenness. Researcher proposes that the formation of solidarity leads to transformation. Yet this remains only a Church language. There is a necessity to translation of the Church vocabulary to a larger community in the context of cyberspace that speak the gospel language of hope, of compassion, of community, of journeying towards a *telos.* It is to include the whole Cosmos and ecology and the formation of humans not understood as patronizing position of stewards but Co-Creators, as part of this big cosmos.

---

[286] The term "public theology" was first coined by Martin Marty in 1974 to describe the work of prominent Protestant social ethicist Reinhold Niebuhr. Marty addressed Public Theology as theological reflection not only to the church but also and intentionally to communities (such as the nation) outside the church. David Tracy (b. 1939) has offered a further articulation of public theology by noting that theologians address three publics: the church, the intellectual community (the "academy"), and society at large. The implication, for Tracy, is that Christian theology is in part a dialog with audiences outside the church. As such, theologians must abide by public criteria of rationality and may also draw on sources of truth that are not overtly Christian. Paul Tillich's (1886-1965) theology illustrates this approach. He drew not only on the Christian tradition but also on insights from psychology, philosophy and art. See Sam Powell, "Public Theology," accessed 28 Feb. 2019, https://sampowelldotnet.files.wordpress.com/2015/07/public-theology.pdf.

Human Formation and Mission

Mission understanding as per the authentic Christian human formation is not the conquering, converting prototype. It is the mandate of "Going to the ends of the World..." (Matthew 28:10) without the colonial aspect of expansion or subjugation. Cyberspace helps in understanding the interconnectedness of the Cosmos. It helps in imagining the Kingdom of God where the finitude of humans are affirmed and the ever expansive scope for relationality and intersective spaces remain to be explored to do mission. The resurrection and eschatology makes a new reality of the world present to us as a radical reality. This becomes the mission where there is no set person assigned to do mission as a specialist. It calls for a mission understanding that everyone inhabiting has a mission in search of *Christic* possibilities. It is to offer the reminder of the reality of human beings being made in the Image of God in a forgetful world, to apply the words of Prophet Micah in Mic 6: 8 "...To do justice, and to love kindness and to walk humbly with your God." As humans we are called to fight for justice in the broken space of cyberspace as a mission. To be an embodiment of love and kindness in an estranged and hostile cyberspace. And finally to connect everyone evolving towards the Omega Point, as a journey of love together engaging in *Tikkun Olam* in a fragmented and alienated context.

Conclusion

Reaching the end of study, the researcher has reworked the Created Co-Creator proposal to arrive at an authentic Christian human formation in the context of cyberspace. The methodology of hybridity opened new doors of investigating the theological anthropology and the contexts. Along with Christological formulations the researcher has attempted to reimagine *Ecclesia,* ministry and mission. There is a further need to study the role of sacraments, to reimagine the leadership in the context of *Ecclesiology* and to have secular engagements in the context of Artificial Intelligence (AI), the world of Robotics, which was not included in the study and was beyond the scope of it. It is important to realize that the cyberspace is a complex phenomenon and the human formation has to constantly engage and dialogue, learn and unlearn. Researcher believes a deeper engagement with Trinity is necessary to expand the premise and the scope of the study as a next phase of the research.

Bibliography

Monographs

Augustine of Hippo. *Greatness of the Soul: The Teacher.* Translated by Joseph M. Colleran. New York: The Newman Press, 1950.

Barth, Karl. "The Covenant as the Internal Basis of Creation." In *Church Dogmatics*, Vol. III/1. Peabody, MA: Hendrickson Publishers, 2010.

Bell, David. *An Introduction to Cybercultures.* New York: Routledge, 2001.

Boellstorff, Tom. *Coming of Age in Second Life: An Anthropologist Explores the Virtually Human.* NJ: Princeton University Press, 2008.

Bolt, John. *Economic Shalom: A Reformed Primer on Faith, Work and Human Flourishing.* Michigan: Christian's Library Press, 2013.

Brock, Brian. *Christian Ethics in a Technological Age.* Michigan: Eerdmans Publishing Company, 2010.

Burns, J. Patout. *Theological Anthropology.* Philadelphia: Fortress Press, 1981.

Clark, Andy. *Natural-Born Cyborgs: Minds, Technologies, and the Future of Human Intelligence.* New York: Oxford University Press, 2003.

Comblin, Jose. *Retreiving the Human: A Christian Anthropology.* Maryknoll: Orbis Books, 1990.

Cortez, Marc. *Christological Anthropology in Historical Perspective: Ancient and Contemporary Approaches to Theological Anthropology.* Michigan: Zondervan, 2016.

_______. *ReSourcing Theological Anthropology: A Constructive Account of Humanity in the Light of Christ.* Michigan: Zondervan, 2017.

_______. *Theological Anthropology: A Guide for the Perplexed.* London: T&T Clark, 2010.

Crossley, Nick. *Social Bodies: Habit, Identity and Desire.* London: Sage Publications, 2001.

Deleuze, Gilles. *Difference and Repetition.* London: Continuum, 2004.

Douglas, Mary. *Purity and Danger: An Analysis of the Concept of Purity and Taboo.* New York: Routledge Classics, 2002.

Erickson, Millard J. *Christian Theology.* Grand Rapids: Baker Book House,1985.

Fern, Richard. *Nature, God and Humanity: Envisioning an Ethics of Nature.* Cambridge: Cambridge University Press, 2002.

Fernandez, Eleazar S. *Reimagining the Human: Theological Anthropology in Response to Systemic Evil.* Missouri: Chalice Press, 2004.

Fukuyama, Francis. *Our Posthuman Future: Consequences of the Biotechnology Revolution.* London: Profile Books, 2003.

Graham, Elaine L. *Representations of the Post/Human: Monsters, Aliens and Others in Popular Culture.* New Jersey: Rutgers University Press, 2002.

Gray, Chris Habbles. *Cyborg Citizen: Politics in Posthuman Age.* New York: Routledge, 2001.

Goizueta, Roberto S. *Caminemos Con Jesus: Toward a Hispanic/Latino Theology of Accompaniment.* New York: Orbis Books, 1995.

Grudum, Wayne. *Business for the Glory of God: The Bible's Teachings on the Moral Goodness of Business*. Illinois: Crossway Books, 2003.

Hakken, David. *Cyborgs@Cyberspace? An Ethnographer Looks to the Future*. New York: Routledge, 1999.

Hamelink, Cees J. *The Ethics of Cyberspace*. New Delhi: Sage Publications, 2000.

Hanh, Thich Nhat. *The Art of Living*. London: Rider, 2017.

Haraway, Donna J. *Modest_Witness@Second_Millennium. Female Man_Meets_OncoMouse: Feminism and Technoscience*. London: Routledge, 1997.

Haraway, Donna J. *Simians, Cyborgs, and Women: The Reinvention of Nature*. New York: Routledge, 1991.

Haraway, Donna J. *The Haraway Reader*. New York: Routledge, 2004.

Harris, John. *Clones, Genes and Immortality*. Oxford: Oxford University Press, 1998.

Hefner, Philip. *The Human Factor: Evolution, Culture and Religion*. Minneapolis: Fortress Press, 1993.

Herzfeld, Noreen. *In Our Image: Artificial Intelligence and the Human Spirit*. Minneapolis: Fortress Press, 2002.

Herzfeld, Noreen. *Technology and Religion: Remaining Human in a Co-created World*. West Conshohocken, PA: Templeton Press, 2009.

Hughes, James. *Citizen Cyborg: Why Democratic Societies Must Respond to the Redesigned Human of the Future*. Cambridge, MA: Westview Press, 2004.

Huyssteen, J. Wentzel van. *Alone in the World? Human Uniqueness in Science and Theology, The Gifford Lectures*. Grand Rapids, MI, 2006.

Kahler, Martin. *So-called Historical Jesus and the Historic, Biblical Christ*. Translated by Carl E. Braaten. Philadelphia: Fortress Press, 1964.

Kesley, David H. *Eccentric Existence: A Theological Anthropology*. Louisville: Westminister John Knox, 2009.

Kurzweil, Ray. *The Singularity is Near: When Humans Transcend Biology*. New York: Penguin Books, 2005.

Latour, Bruno. *We Have Never Been Modern*. Cambridge: Harvard University Press, 1993.

Lewis, Gordon R. and Bruce A. Demarest. *Integrative Theology*, Vol. 2. Grand Rapids, MI: Zondervan, 1996.

Midson, Scott A. *Cyborg Theology: Humans Technology and God*. London: I.B. Tauris, 2018.

Mitchell, William. *Me++: The Cyborg Self and the Network City*. Cambridge: MIT Press, 1998.

Moltmann, Jürgen. *The Coming of God*. Translated by Margaret Kohl. Minneapolis: Fortress Press, 1996.

Nayar, Pramod K. *Posthumanism*. Cambridge/Malden, MA: Polity Press, 2014.

Nungshitula, *The Naga Images of Human Being: A Resource for Contemporary Theological Anthropology*. Jorhat: Tribal Study Centre, 2001.

Pasnau, Robert. *Thomas Aquinas On Human Nature*. Cambridge: Cambridge University Press, 2002.

Peacocke, Arthur R. *God and the New Biology*. London: Dent, 1986.

Peters, Ted. *Playing God? Genetic Determinism and Human Freedom* New York and London: Routledge, 2003.

Rad, Gerhard Von. *Genesis: A Commentary*. Philadelphia, PA: The Westminister Press, 1972.

Schneider, Joseph. *Donna Haraway: Live Theory*. New York: Continuum, 2005.

Scott, Peter. *Anti-Human Theology: Nature, Technology and the Postnatural*. London: SCM Press, 2010.

Shirky, Clay. *Here Comes Everybody: The Power of Organizing without Organizations*. New York: Penguin, 2008.

Shults, F. LeRon. *Christology and Science*. Grand Rapids, MI, 2008.

______. *Reforming Theological Anthropology: After Philosophical Turn to Relationality.* Grand Rapids: Abingdon Press, 2003.

Spadaro, Antonio. *Cybertheology: Thinking Christianity in the Era of the Internet.* New York: Fordham University Press, 2014.

Taylor, Charles. *A Secular Age* (Massachusetts: The Benkalp Press of Harvard University Press, 2007.

Taylor, T. L. *Play Between Worlds: Exploring Online Game Culture.* Cambridge, MA: MIT Press, 2006.

Teilhard de Chardin, Pierre. *The Phenomenon of Man.* New York: Harper and Row, 1976.

Thweatt-Bates, Jeanine. *Cyborg Selves: A Theological Anthropology of the Posthuman.* London and New York: Routledge, Taylor and Francis Group, 2012.

Turkle, Sherry. *Life on the Screen: Identity in the Age of the Internet.* New York: Touchstone Books, 1996.

Wagner, Sven. *The Scientist as God: A Typological Study of Literary Motif, 1818 to the Present.* Heidelberg: Universitatverlag Winter Heidelberg, 2012.

Warwick, Stephen. *I, Cyborg.* London: University of Reading Press, 2000.

Waters, Brent. *From Human to Posthuman: Christian Theology and Technology in a Postmodern World.* Hampshire: Ashgate, 2006.

Wolfe, Cary. *What is Posthumanism?* Minneapolis: University of Minnesota Press, 2009.

World Council of Churches. *Christian Perspectives on Theological Anthropology: A Faith and Order Paper, no.199.* Geneva: World Council of Churches, 2005.

Young, Simon. *Designer Evolution: A Transhumanist Manifesto.* New York: Prometheus Books, 2006.

Articles in Books

Brazal, Agnes M. "A Cyborg Spirituality and Its Theo-Anthropological Foundation." In *Feminist Cyberethics in Asia:*

Religious Discourses in Connectivity. Edited by Agnes M. Brazal and Kochurani Abraham. New York: Palgrave Macmillan, 2014.

Bostrom, Nick. "Introduction-The Transhumanist FAQ: A General Introduction." In *Transhumanism and the Body: The World Religion Speaks*. Edited by Calvin Mercer and Derek F. Maher. New York: Palgrave Macmillan, 2004.

Coombes, Annie and Avtar Brah. "Introduction: The Conundrum of Mixing." In *Hybridity and its Discontents: Politics, Science, Culture*. Edited by Avtar Brah and Annie Coombes. New York: Routledge, 2000.

Clynes, Manfred and Nathan S. Kline. "Cyborgs in Space." In *The Cyborg Handbook*. Edited by Chris Hables Gray. New York: Routledge, 1995.

Dawson, L. L. "Researching Religion in Cyberspace: Issues and Strategies." In *Religion on the Internet: Research Prospects and Promises*. Edited by J. K. Hadden and D. E. Cowan. New York: Elsevier Science, 2000.

Edwards, Denis "Discovery of Chaos and the Retrieval of Trinity." In *Chaos and Complexity Scientific Perspectives on Divine Action*. Edited by Robert John Russel, Nancey Murphy and Arthur R. Peacocke. Vatican City State: Vatican Observatory Publications, and Berkeley: Center for Theology and Natural Sciences, 1995.

Edwards, Denis. "Teilhard's Vision As Agenda for Rahner's Christology." In *From Teilhard to Omega: Co-Creating an Unfinished Universe*. Edited by Ilia Delio. Bangalore: Theological Publication of India, 2014.

Garner, Stephen. "The Hopeful Cyborg." In *Transhumanism and Transcendence: Christian Hope in an Age of Technological Enhancement*. Edited by Ronald Cole-Turner. Washington, DC: Georgetown University Press, 2011.

González, Jennifer. "Envisioning Cyborg Bodies: Notes from Current Research." In *The Cyborg Handbook*. Edited by Chris Hables Gray. London: Routledge, 1995.

Haraway, Donna J. "A Cyborg Manifesto: Science, Technology and Socialist-Feminism in the Late Twentieth Century." In *The*

Cybercultures Reader. Edited by David Bell and Barbara M. Kennedy. London, New York: Routledge, 2000.

________. "Mice Into Wormholes: A Comment on the Nature of No Nature." In Cyborgs *& Citadels: Anthropological Interventions in Emerging Sciences and Technologies.* Edited by G. L. Downey and J. Dumit. New Mexico: School of American Research Press, 1997.

Hefner, Philip. "*Imago Dei:* The Possibility and Necessity of the Human Person." In *The Human Person in Science and Theology*. Edited by Niels Henrik Gregersen, Willem B. Drees, and Ulf Gorman. Edinburgh: T&T Clark, 2000.

________. "The Evolution of the Created Co-Creator." In *Cosmos as Creation: Theology and Science in Consonance*. Edited by Ted Peters. Nashville: Abingdon Press, 1989.

Kadaplackal, Francis. "In Search of an Adequate Christian Anthropology." In *Technology, Trust, and Religion: Roles of Religions in Controversies on Ecology and the Modification of Life*. Edited by Willem B. Drees. Amsterdam: Leiden University Press, 2009.

Kesley, David H. "Human Being" in *Christian Theology: An Introduction to its Traditions and Tasks*. Edited by Peter C. Hodgson and Robert H. King. Philadelphia: Fortress Press, 1986.

Latour, Bruno. "Where Are the Missing Masses? The Sociology of Few Mundane Artefacts." In *Shaping Technology/Building Society: Studies in Sociotechnical Change*. Edited by Wiebe E. Bijker & John Law. Cambridge, MA.: MIT Press, 1992.

Merrill, Eugene H. "Image of God." In *Dictionary of the Old Testament: Pentateuch*. Edited by T. Desmond Alexander and David W. Baker. Downers Grove, IL: InterVarsity Press, 2003.

Rade-Antweiler, Kerstin. "Authenticity" in *Digital Religion: Understanding Religious Practice in New Media World.* Edited by Heidi A. Campbell. New York: Routledge, 2013.

Tillich, Paul. "The Technical City as Symbol." In *Tillich, The Spiritual Situation in Our Technical Society*. Edited by J. Mark Thomas. Macon: Mercer University Press, 1988.

Journals and Periodicals

Case-Winters, Anna. 'Rethinking the Image of God' *Zygon: Journal of Religion and Science.* Vol. 39, No. 4 (December 2004): 813-826.

Couenhoven, Jesse. "St. Augustine's Doctrine of Original Sin." *Augustinian Studies* 36:2 (2005): 359–396.

Doncel, Manuel G. "The Kenosis of the Creator and the Created Co-Creator." *Zygon* Vol. 39, No. 4 (December 2004): 791-800.

Fergusson, David. "Humans Created according to the *Imago Dei*: An Alternative Proposal." *Zygon* Vol. 48, No. 2 (2013): 439-453.

Geraci, Robert. "Robots and the Sacred in Science and Science Fiction: Theological Implications of Artificial Intelligence." *Zygon* Vol. 42, No. 4 (Dec 2007): 961-980.

Grenz, Stanley J. "Jesus As The *Imago Dei*: Image-of-God Christology and the Non-Linear Linearity of Theology." *Journal of Evangelical Society 47/4* (December 2004): 609-634.

Gupta, Ankur. "Peer-To-Peer Networks and Computation: Current Trends and Future Perspectives." *Computing and Informatics* Vol. 30, (2011): 559–594.

Haugen, Joe E. "The Theological Anthropology of Ralph Wendell Burhoe." *Zygon.* Vol. 30, No. 4 (December 1995): 547-561.

Hefner, Philip. "Biocultural Evolution of the Created Co-Creator." *Dialog: A Journal of Theology* Vol. 36, No. 2 (1997): 197-205.

________. "Can the Created Co-Creator Be Lutheran?" *Dialog: A Journal of Theology.* Vol. 44, No. 1, (2005): 184-188.

Kline, Ronald. "Where are the Cyborg in Cybernetics?" *Social Studies of Science* 39/3 (June 2009): 331–362.

Kull, Anne. 'The Cyborg as an Interpretation of Culture-Nature.' *Zygon.* Vol. 36, No. 1 (March 2001): 49-56.

Latour, Bruno. "On Interobjectivity." In *Mind, Culture, and Activity.* Vol. 3, No. 4, (1996): 228-245.

Marasigan, Vincent. "Teilhard Recalled." *Landas* Vol. 11 (1997): 198-202.

Mbanaso, U. M. "The Cyberspace: Redefining A New World." *IOSR Journal of Computer Engineering.* (IOSR-JCE) Volume 17, Issue 3, Ver. VI. (May – Jun. 2015): 17-24.

Peters, Ted. "Techno-Secularism, Religion and the Created Co-Creator." *Zygon.* Vol. 40, No. 4. (2005): 845-862.

Peterson, Gregory R. "Imaging God: Cyborgs, Brain-Machine Interfaces, and a More Human Future." *Dialog* Vol. 44, No. 4 (2005): 337-346.

Peterson, Gregory R. "The Created Co-Creator: What it is and is not." *Zygon.* Vol. 39 No. 4 (2004): 827-840.

Russell, Robert John. "Five Attitudes toward Nature and Technology from a Christian Perspective." *Theology and Science* 1. No. 2 (October 2003): 149-159.

Samartha, S. J. "Images of the Human: A Search for Wholeness." *Asian Journal of Theology.* Vol. 8, No. 2. (October 1994): 255-272.

Stephenson, Bret. "Nature, Technology and the *Imago Dei*: Mediating the Nonhuman through the Practice of Science." *Perspectives on Science and Christian Faith.* Vol. 57, No. 1 (2005): 6-12.

Tosello, Mario E. "Performing Cyberspace: Dance, Technology and Virtual Architecture", International Journal of Architectural Computing, Issue 03, Vol. 01, (2003): 393-413.

Westhelle, Vítor. "The Poet, Practioner and Beholder: Remarks on Hefner's Created Co-Creator." *Zygon.* Vol. 39, No. 4 (December 2004): 747-754.

Willer, Roger A. "Created Co-Creator in the Perspective of Church and Ethics." *Zygon.* Vol. 39 No. 4 (2004): 841-858.

Unpublished Thesis

Ferrando, Francesca. "The Posthuman: Philosophical Posthumanism and Its Others." Ph.D. dissertation, Università di Roma Tre, 2014.

Garner, Stephen. "Transhumanism and the *Imago Dei*: Narratives of Apprehension and Hope." Ph.D. dissertation, The University of Auckland, 2006.

Guridi, Roman. "Imago Dei as Kenosis: Re-imagining Humanity in an Ecological Era." Ph.D. dissertation, Boston College, School of Theology and Ministry, 2016.

Kim, Dai Sil. "Doctrine of Man in Irenaeus of Lyons." Ph.D. dissertation, Boston University, School of Theology, 1969.

Lidums, Gatis. "The Doctrine of *Imago Dei* and Its Relation To Self-Transcendence In The Context of Practical Theology." Ph.D. dissertation, Faculty of Theology of the University of Helsinki, 2004.

Midson, Scott A. "The Cyborg and the Human: Origins, Creatureliness and Hybridity in Theological Anthropology." Ph.D. dissertation, University of Manchester, 2015.

Nishant Shah, "The Technosocial Subject: Cities, Cyborgs and Cyberspace." Ph.D. dissertation, Manipal University, 2012.

Paul, Jason Roberts. "Emerging in the Image of God: From Evolution to Ethics in a Second Naïveté Understanding of Christian Anthropology." Ph.D. dissertation, Marquette University, 2009.

Webliography (Electronic Sources)

"Bioconservatives." Accessed 16 Jan. 2019. https://ieet.org/index.php/tpwiki/Bioconservative/.

Bostrom, Nick. *The Transhumanist FAQ: A General Introduction, Version 2.1.* World Transhumanist Association, October 2003. Accessed 3 Nov. 2019. http://transhumanism.org/resources/FAQv21.pdf.

Cortez, Marc. "Vocationalizing the *Imago Dei.*" Accessed 25 Jan. 2019. https://www.wheaton.edu/media/opus/Cortez–Vocationalizing-the-imago-Dei.pdf.

"Frankenstein." In *English Oxford Living Dictionaries.* Accessed 28 Feb. 2019. https://en.oxforddictionaries.com/definition/frankenstein.

Freeman, Tzvi. "What Is Tikkun Olam," *Chabad.Org*. Accessed 28 Feb 2019. https://www.chabad.org/library/article_cdo/aid/3700275/jewish/What-Is-Tikkun-Olam.htm.

Garner, Stephen. "Living in the Borderlands: Cyborgs and the *Imago Dei.*" Accessed 25 Jan. 2019. https://www.researchgate.net/publication/242247017_Living_in_the_Borderlands_Cyborgs_and_the_Imago_Dei.

Hefner, Philip. "Created Co-Creator Meets Cyborg." Accessed 21 Nov. 2018. https://www.metanexus.net/created-co-creator-meets-cyborg/.

Hughes, James. "Democratic Transhumanism 2.0." Institute for Ethics and Emerging Technologies. Accessed 3 Nov. 2018. https://ieet.org/index.php/IEET2/print/1339.

"Human/Non-Human Chimeras." In *Stanford Encyclopedia of Philosophy.* Accessed 13 Dec. 2018. https://plato.stanford.edu/entries/chimeras/.

"Hybrid." Accessed 5 Feb. 2019. www.vocabulary.com/dictionary/hybrid.

"Hylomorphism." In *Encyclopedia Britannica.* Accessed 13 Nov. 2018. https://www.britannica.com/topic/hylomorphism.

Kinsinger, Frank Stuart. "Beneficence and the Professional's Moral Imperative." *Elsevier* (1st April 2010) Accessed 7 Mar. 2019. https://www.ncbi.nlm.nih.gov/pmc/articles/PMC3342811/.

Kadaplackal, Francis. "Created Co-Creator as a Source of Inspiration for a Sustainable Corporate Environmental Responsibility." Accessed 20 Jan. 2019. https://www.stthomas.edu/media/cleanupfolder/KadaplackalFinalpa.pdf.

"Nanobots." Accessed 23 Jan. 2019. https://www.techopedia.com/definition/8494/nanobot.

"Neoplatonism." In *Stanford Encyclopedia of Philosophy.* Accessed 13 Nov. 2018. https://plato.stanford.edu/entries/neoplatonism/.

Powell, Sam. "Public Theology." Accessed 28 Feb. 2019, https://sampowelldotnet.files.wordpress.com/2015/07/public-theology.pdf.

Reedy, Christina. "Kurzweil Claims That the Singularity Will Happen by 2045," *Future Society.* 5 October 2017. Accessed 23 Jan. 2019. https://futurism.com/kurzweil-claims-that-the-singularity-will-happen-by-2045.

"Substance." In *Stanford Encyclopedia of Philosophy.* Accessed 13 Nov. 2018. https://plato.stanford.edu/entries/substance/.

Slick, Matt. "What is Theosis," *CARM.* Accessed 7 Mar. 2019. https://carm.org/what-is-theosis.

Swirnbine, Richard. "The Coherence ofThe Chalcedonian Definition of the Incarnation." Accessed 7 Mar. 2019. http://users.ox.ac.uk/~orie0087/pdf_files/Papers%20from%20Philosophical%20Journals/Swinburne_2011-incarnation.pdf.

"Telenomy." Accessed 17 Nov 2018. https://en.wikipedia.org/wiki/Teleonomy.

"Transhumanist FAQ." Accessed 26 Feb 2019. https://hpluspedia.org/wiki/Transhumanist_FAQ.

Vinge, Vernor. "The Coming Technological Singularity," *Whole Earth Review* Winter (1993). Accessed 18 Nov. 2018. www.ugcs.caltech.edu/-pheonix/vinge/vinge-sing.html.

Vold, Karina. "Are 'you' just inside your skin or is your smartphone part of you?" *Aeon*, 26 February 2018. Accessed 18 November 2018. https://aeon.co/ideas/are-you-just-inside-your-skin-or-is-your-smartphone-part-of-you.

Wright, N. T. "Jesus Is Coming: Plant a Tree." Accessed 29 Jan 2019. https://www.plough.com/en/topics/justice/environment/jesus-is-coming-plant-a-tree.